SOPHIA RAUCH   SCANS AT HOME

I0483339

Sophia Rauch
Born 1984 in Berkeley, California
Lives and works in Brooklyn, New York

ISBN 978-0-9916493-3-4

Designed & Published by FLTFL, North Andover, Massachusetts / WWW.FLTFL.COM

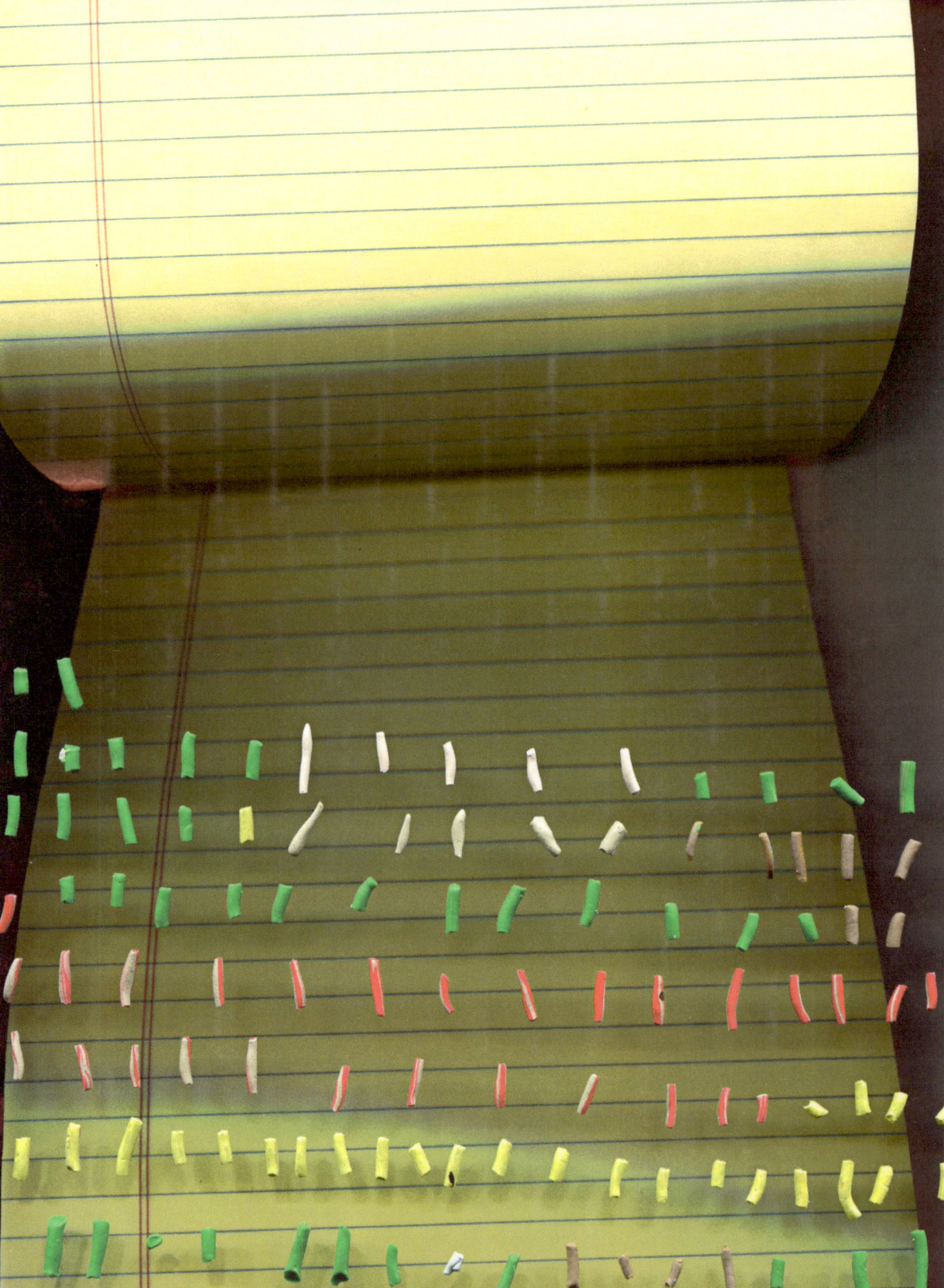

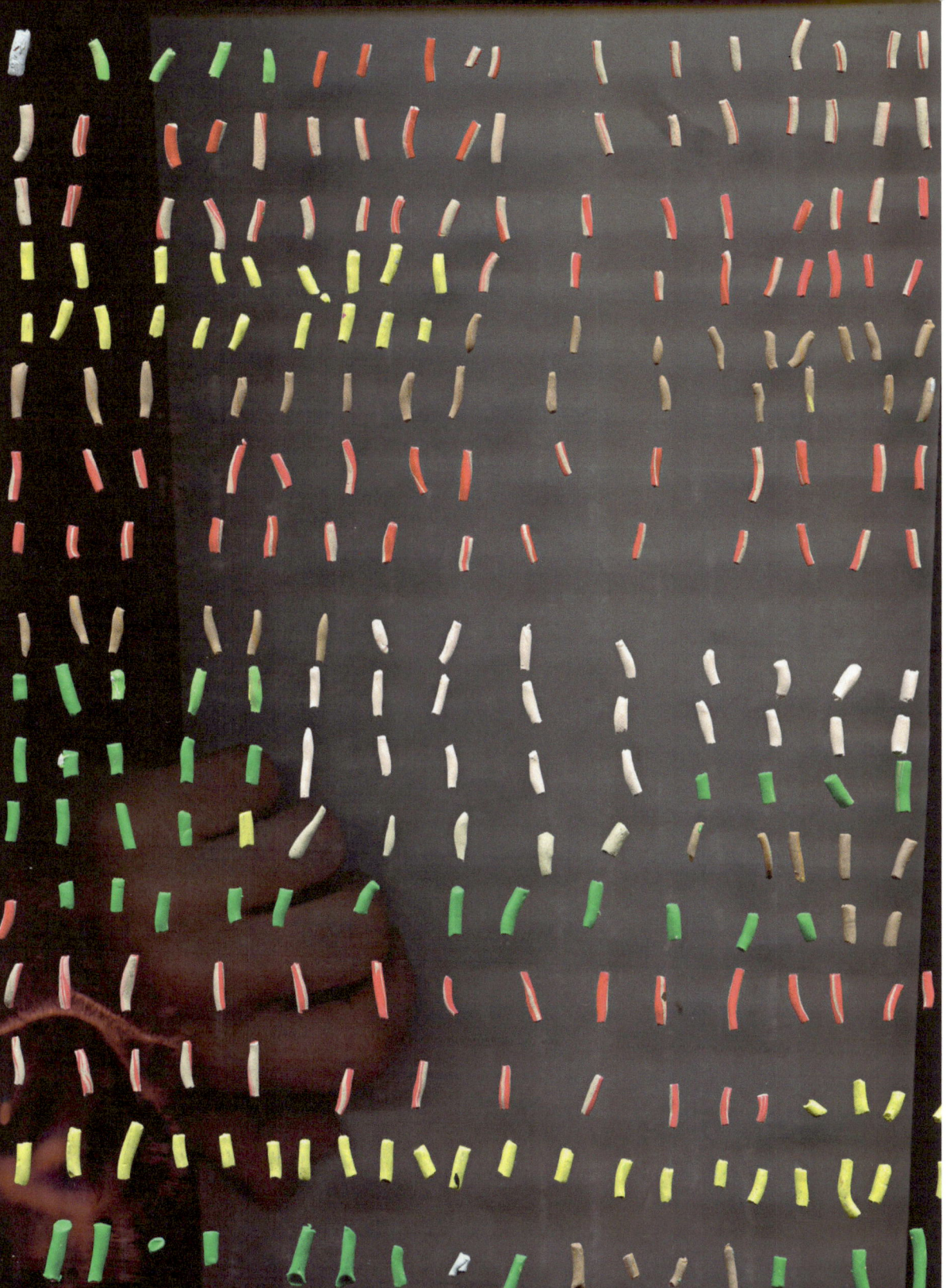

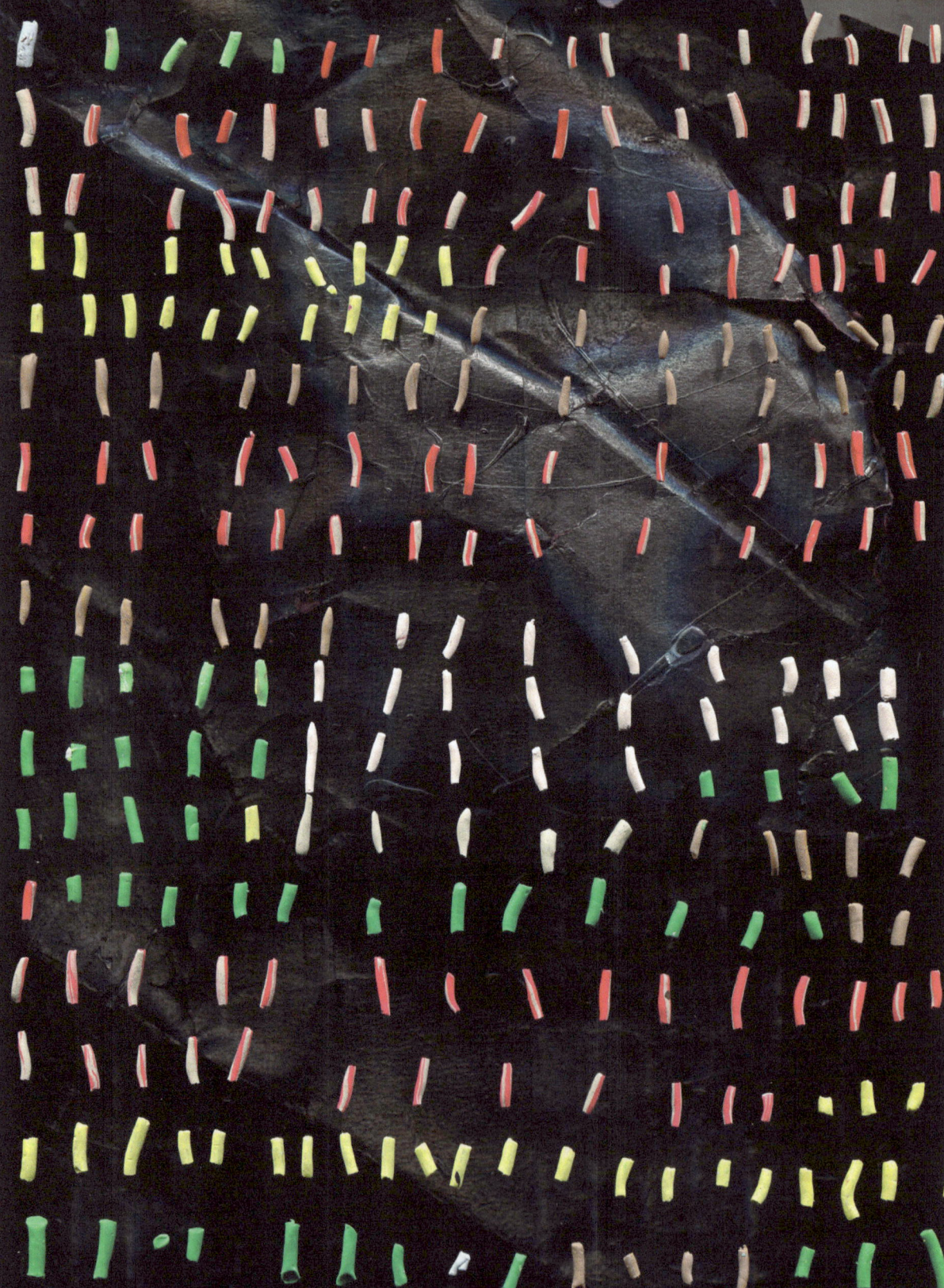

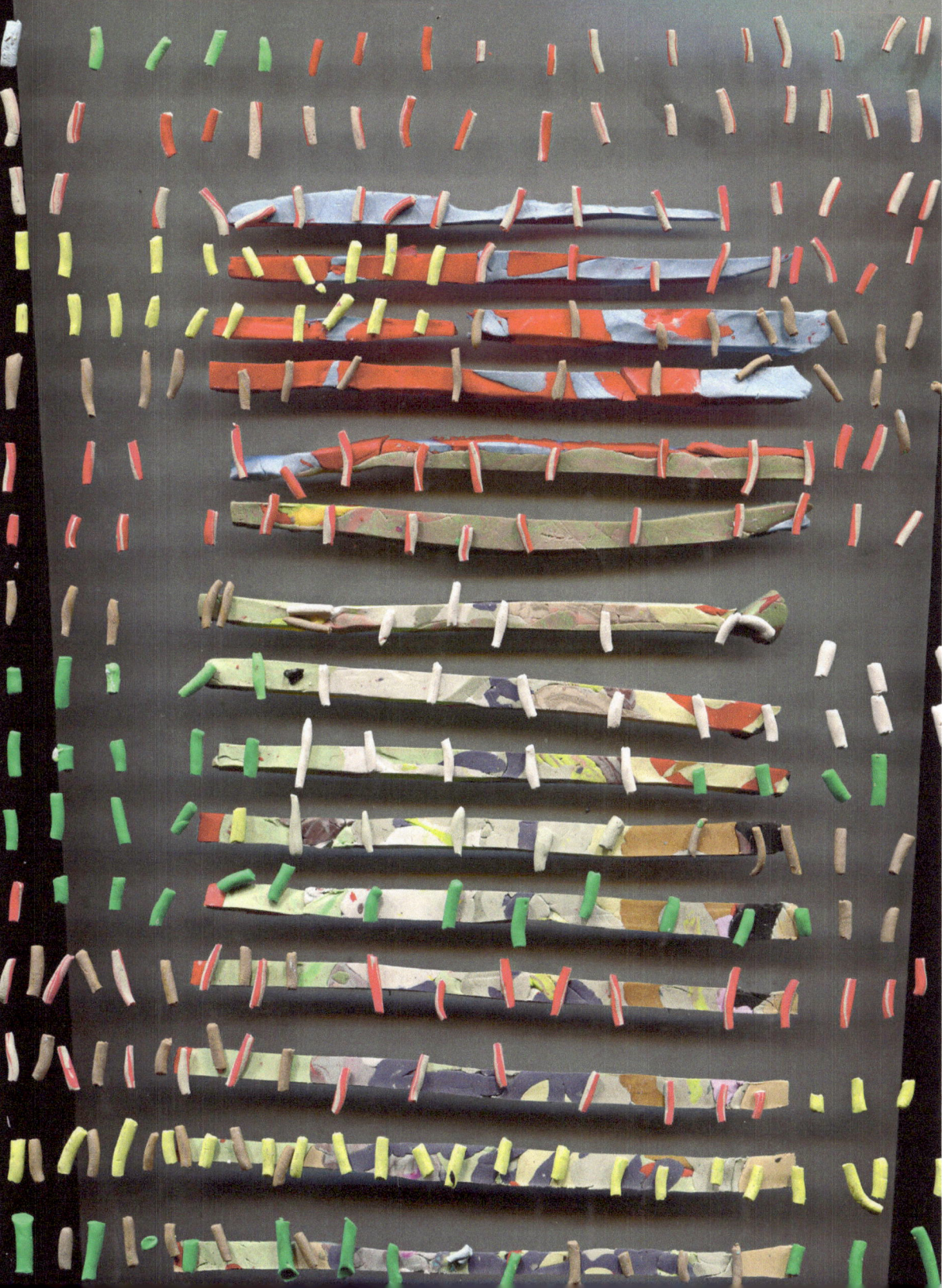

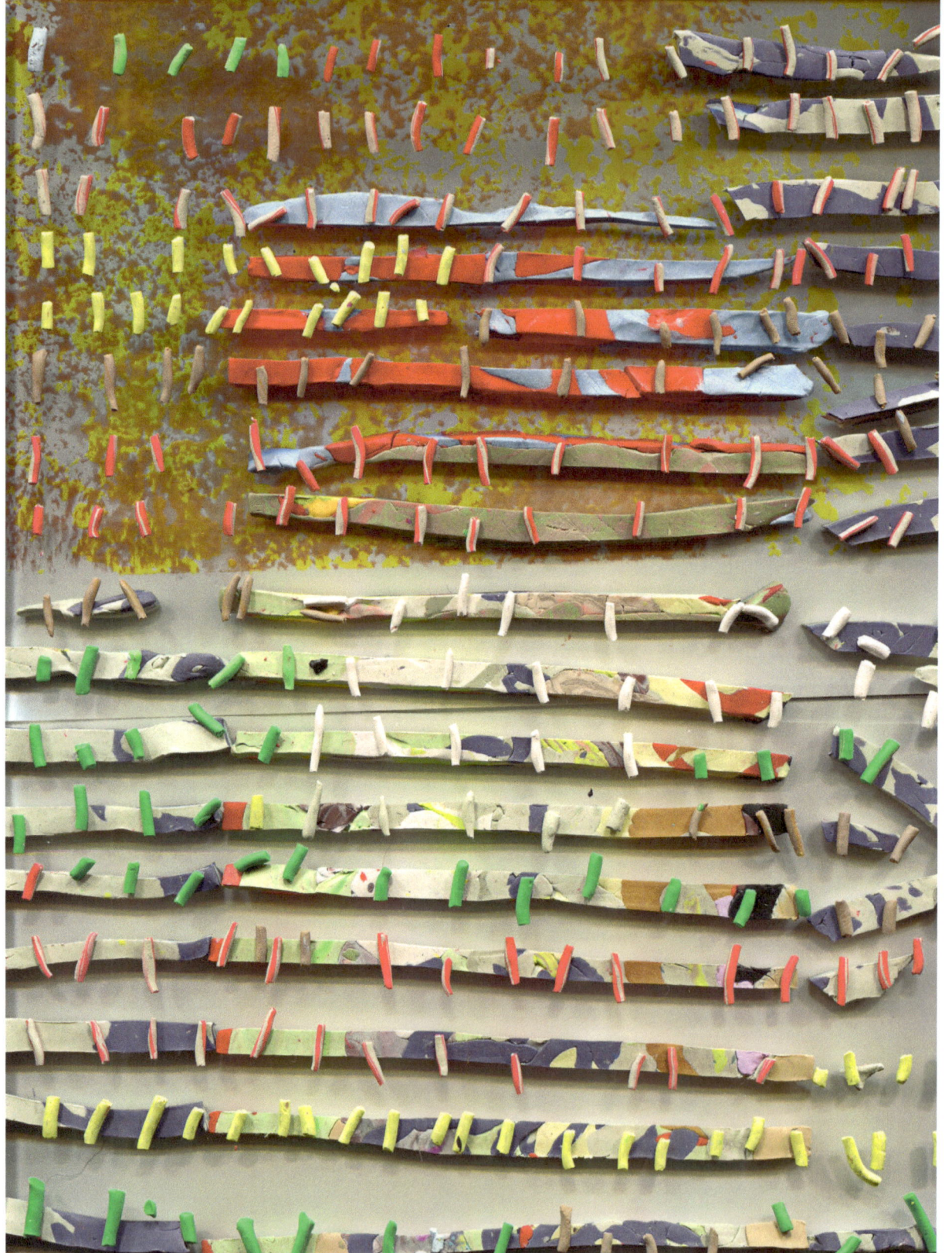

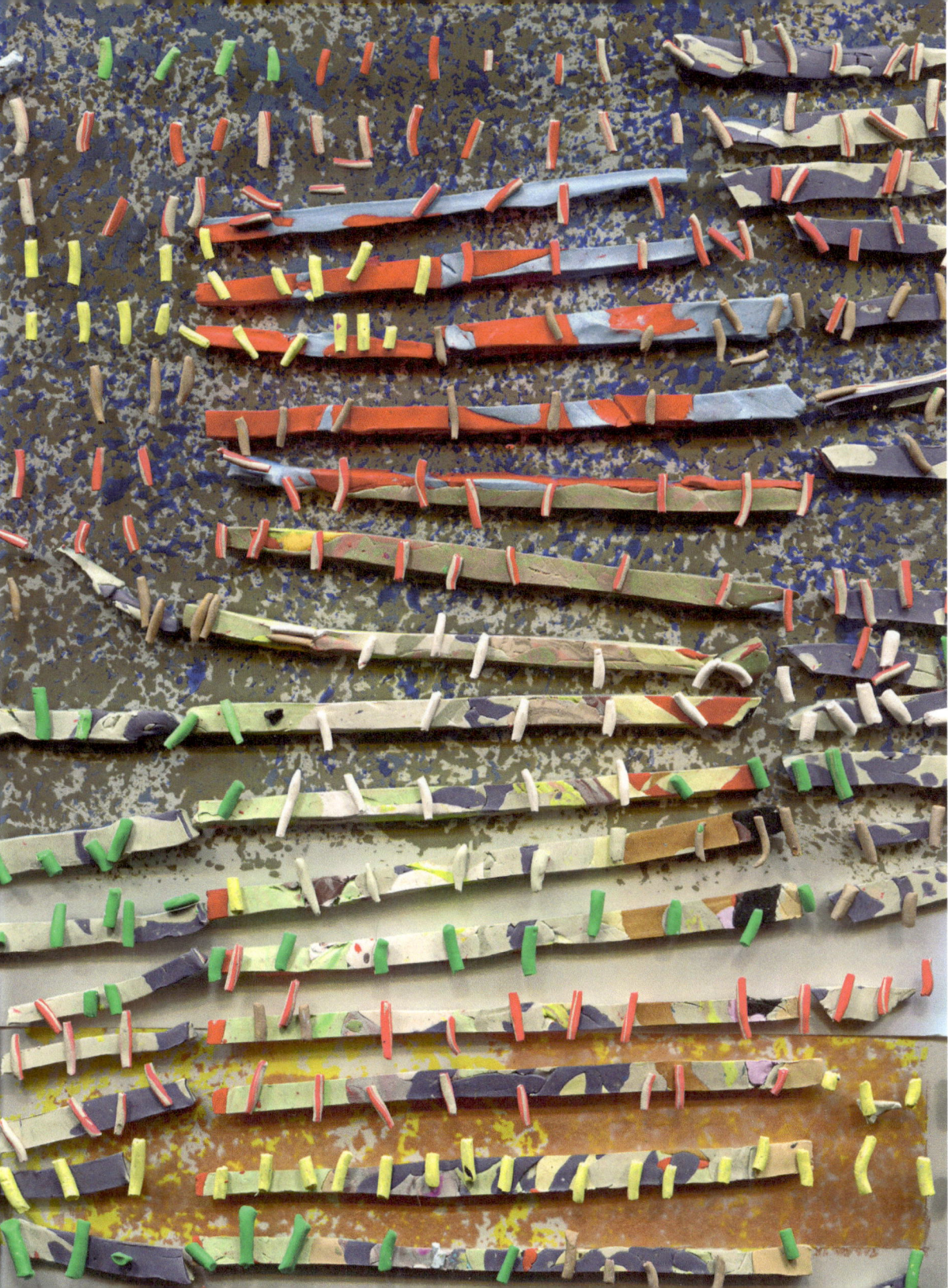

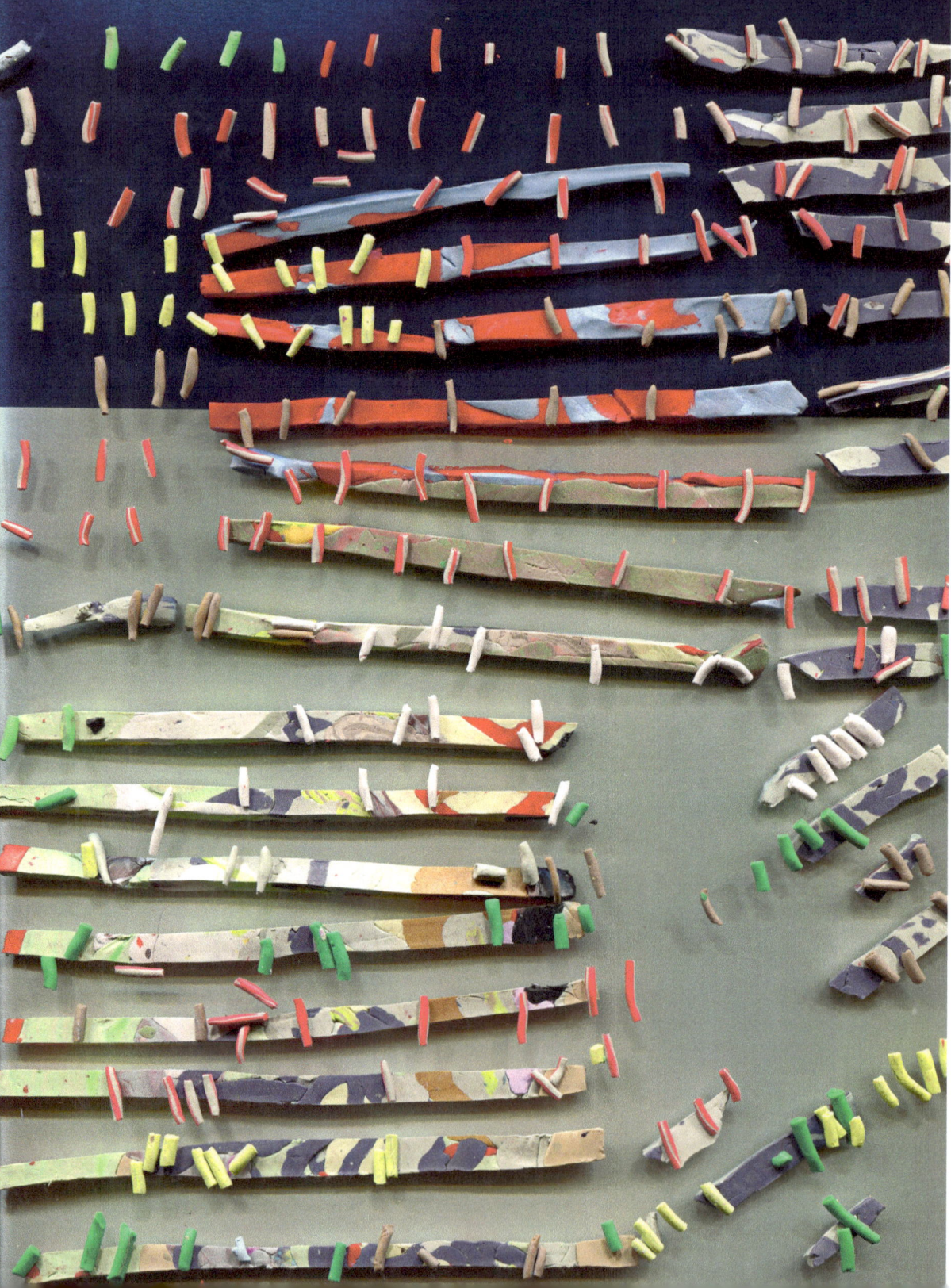

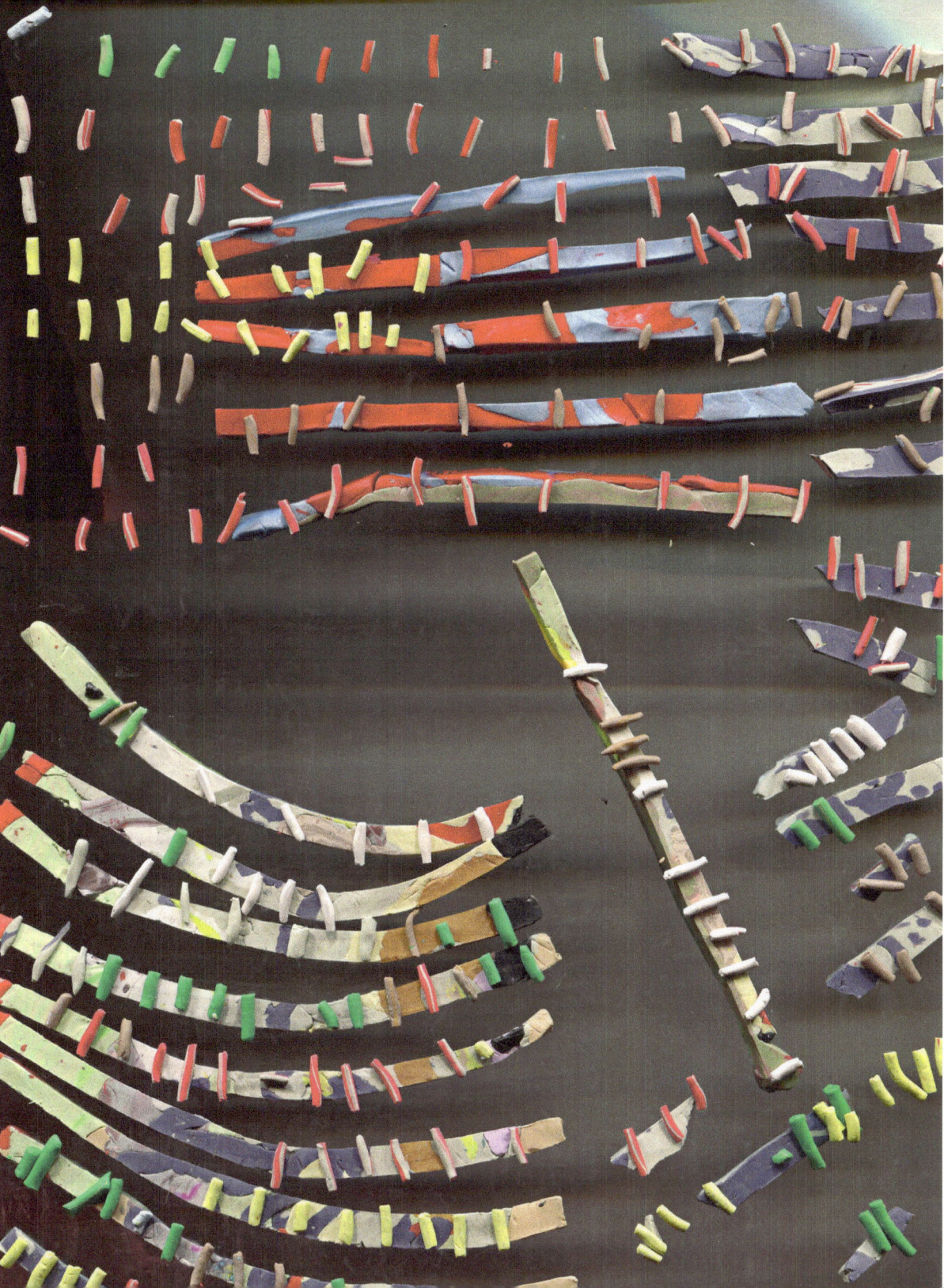

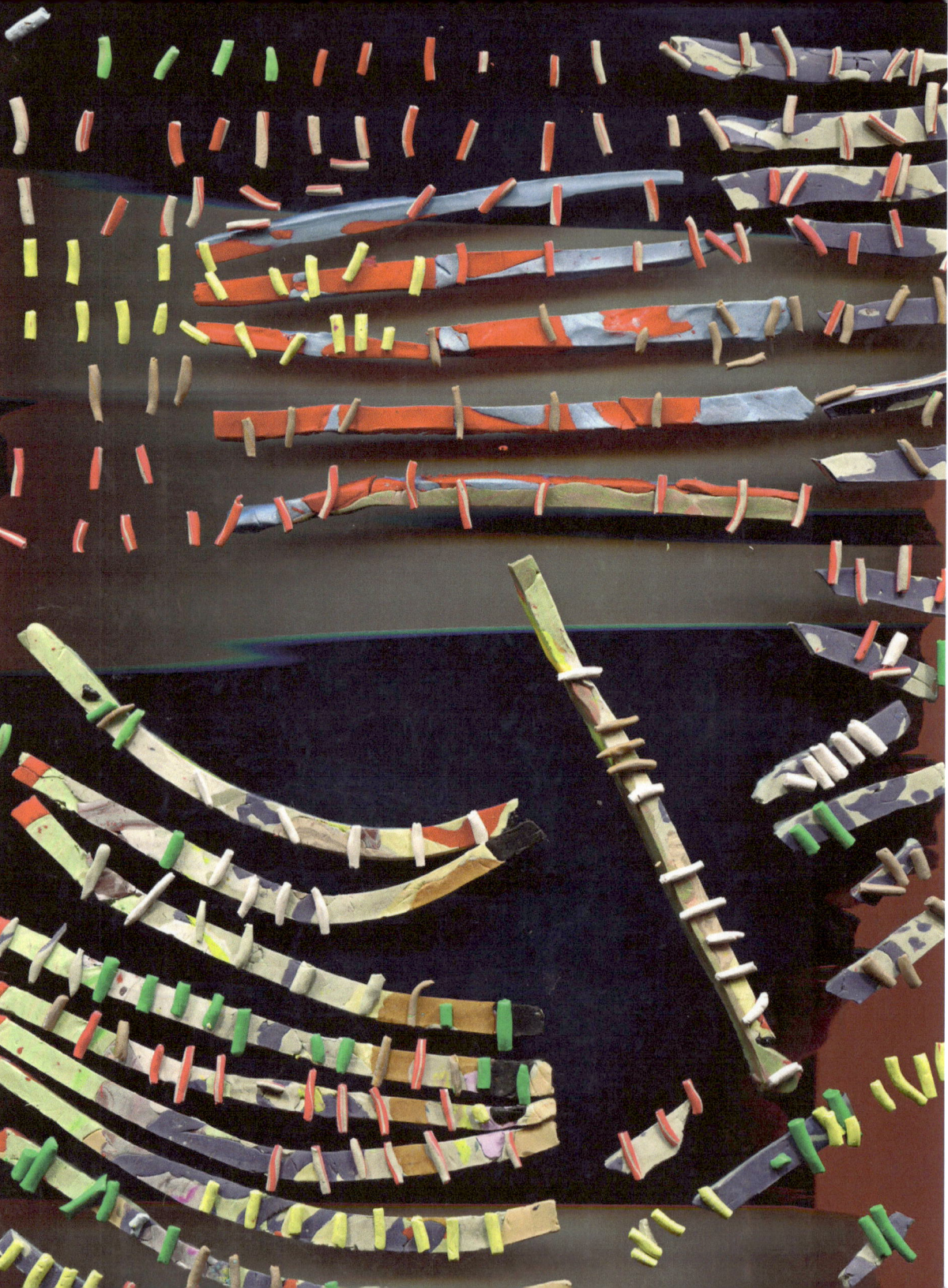

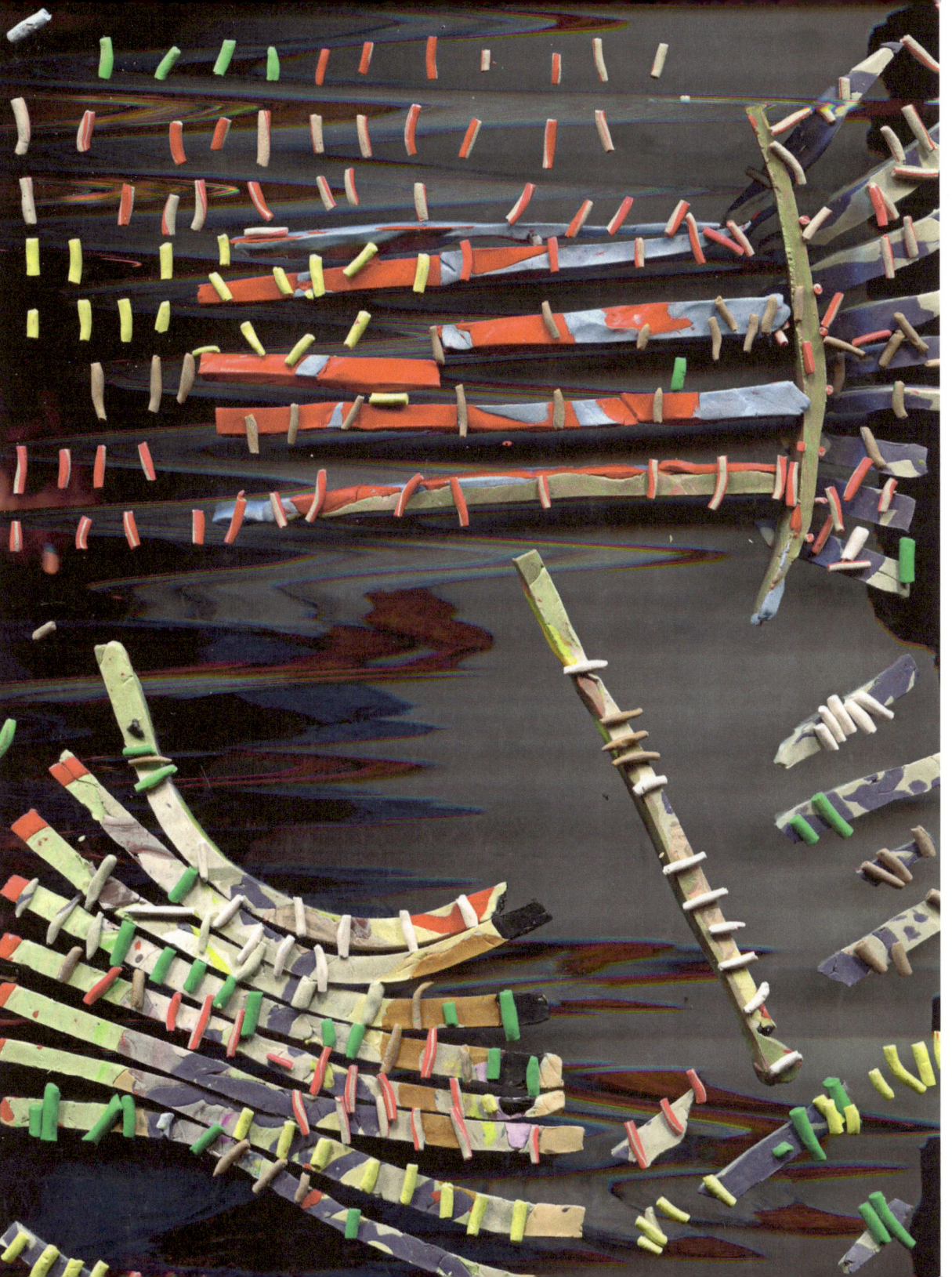

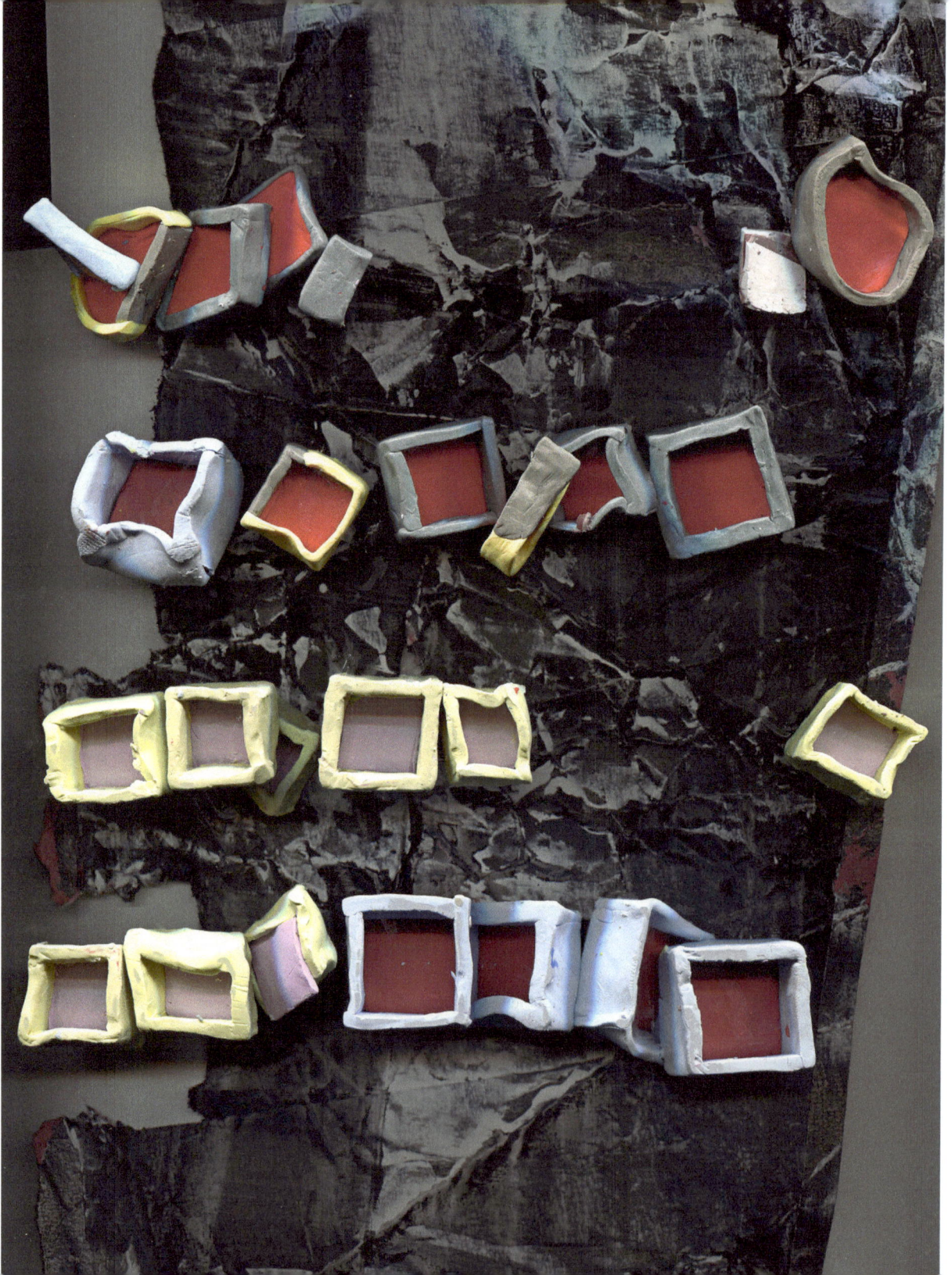

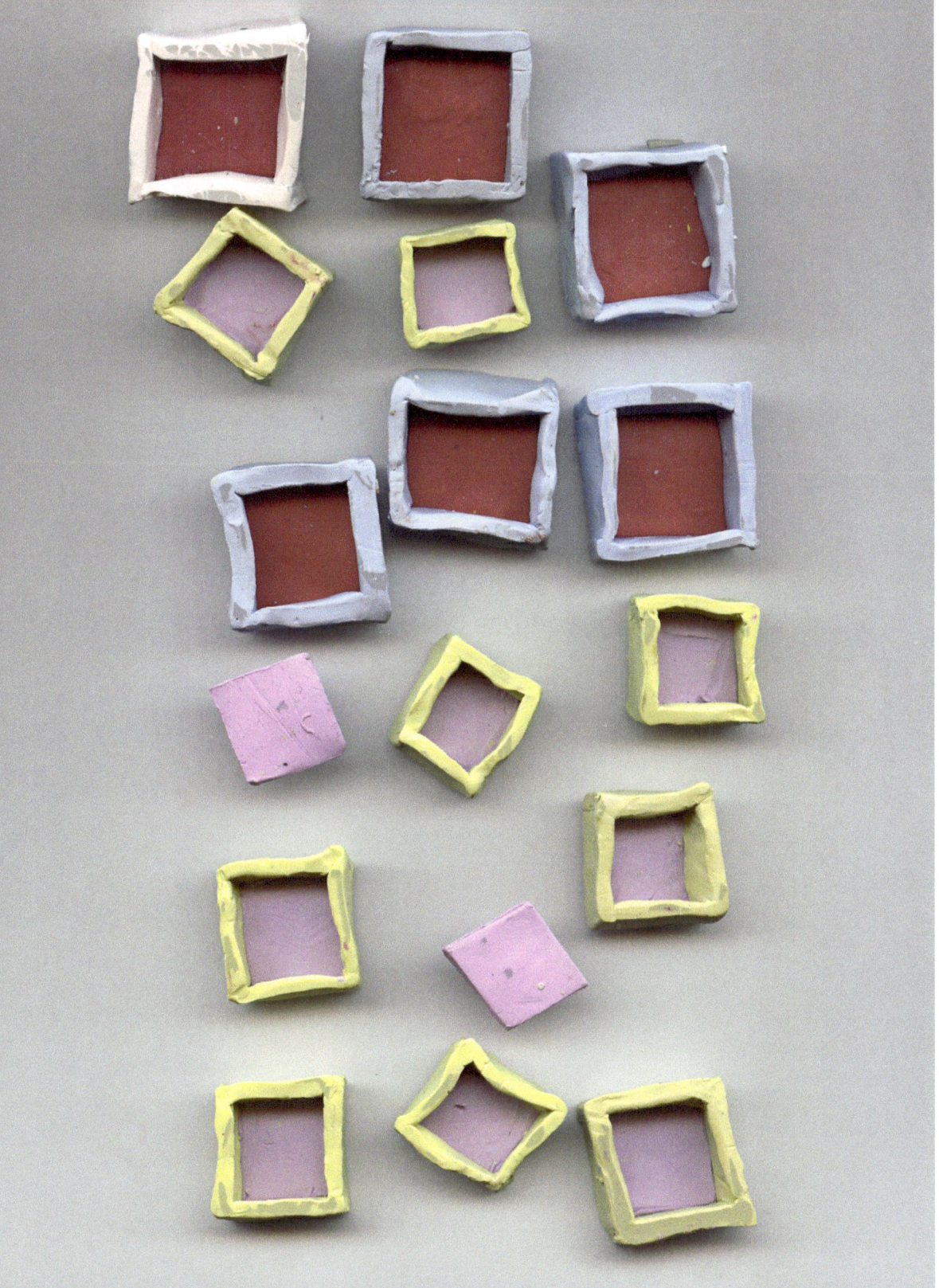

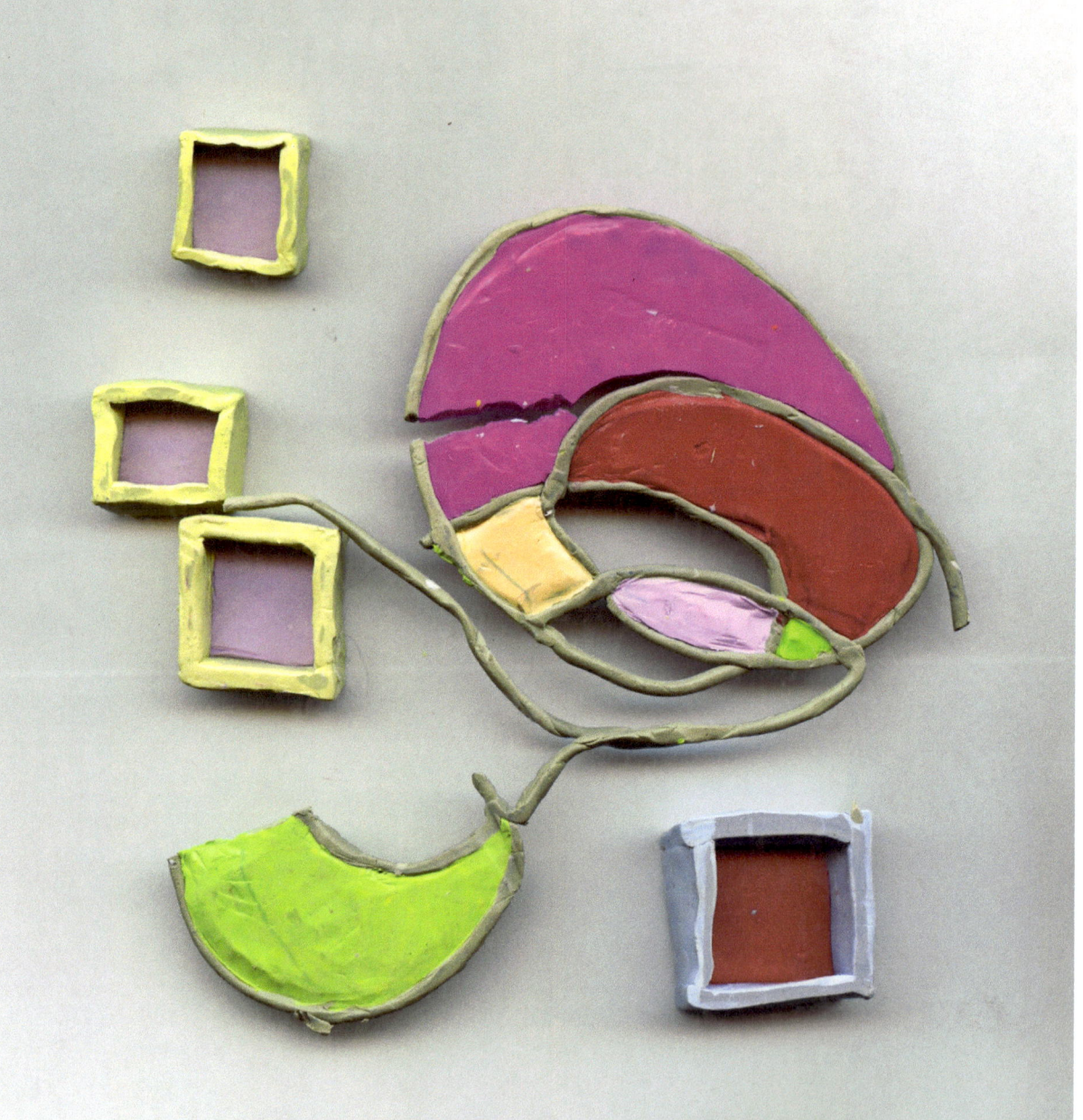

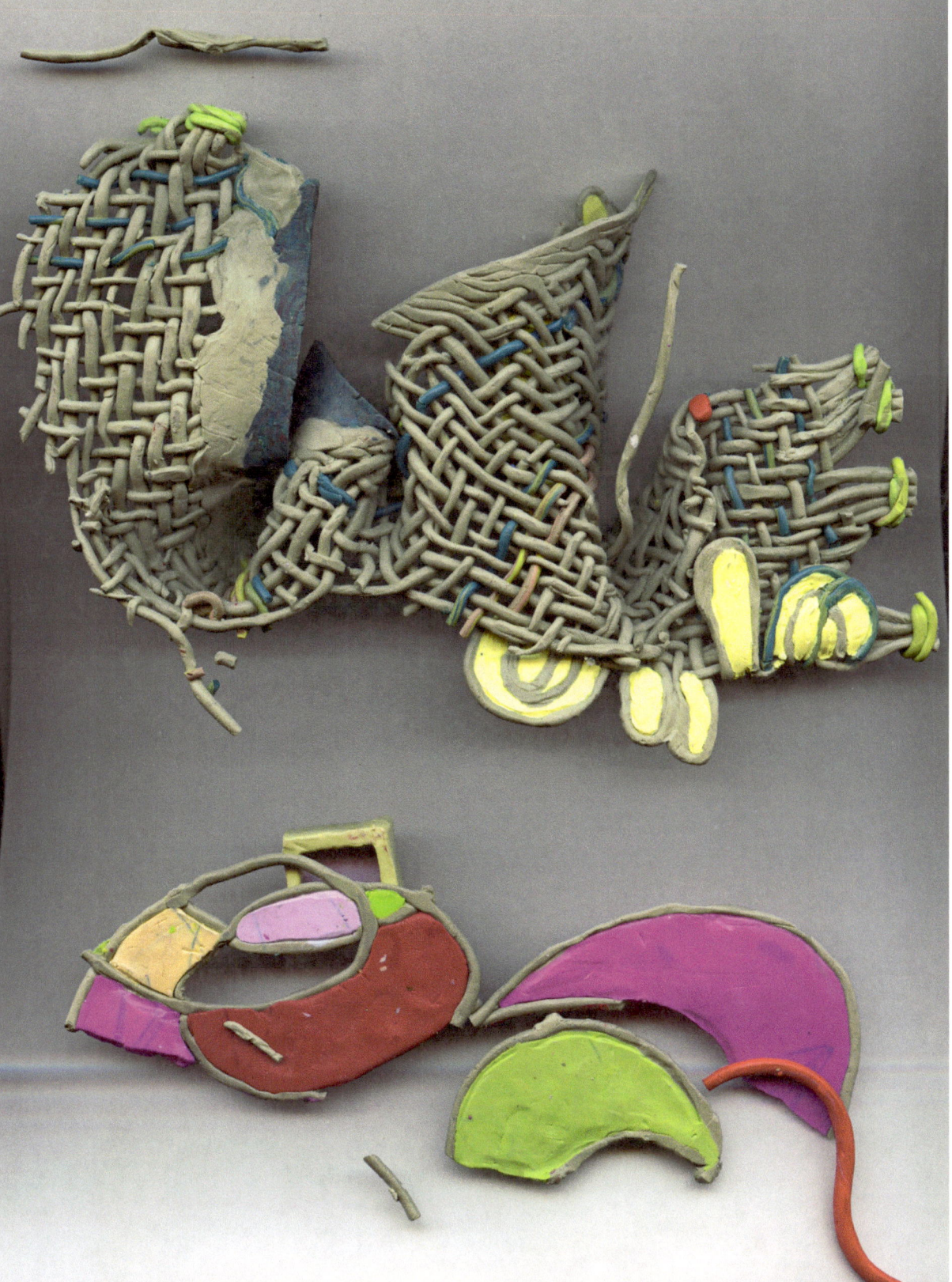

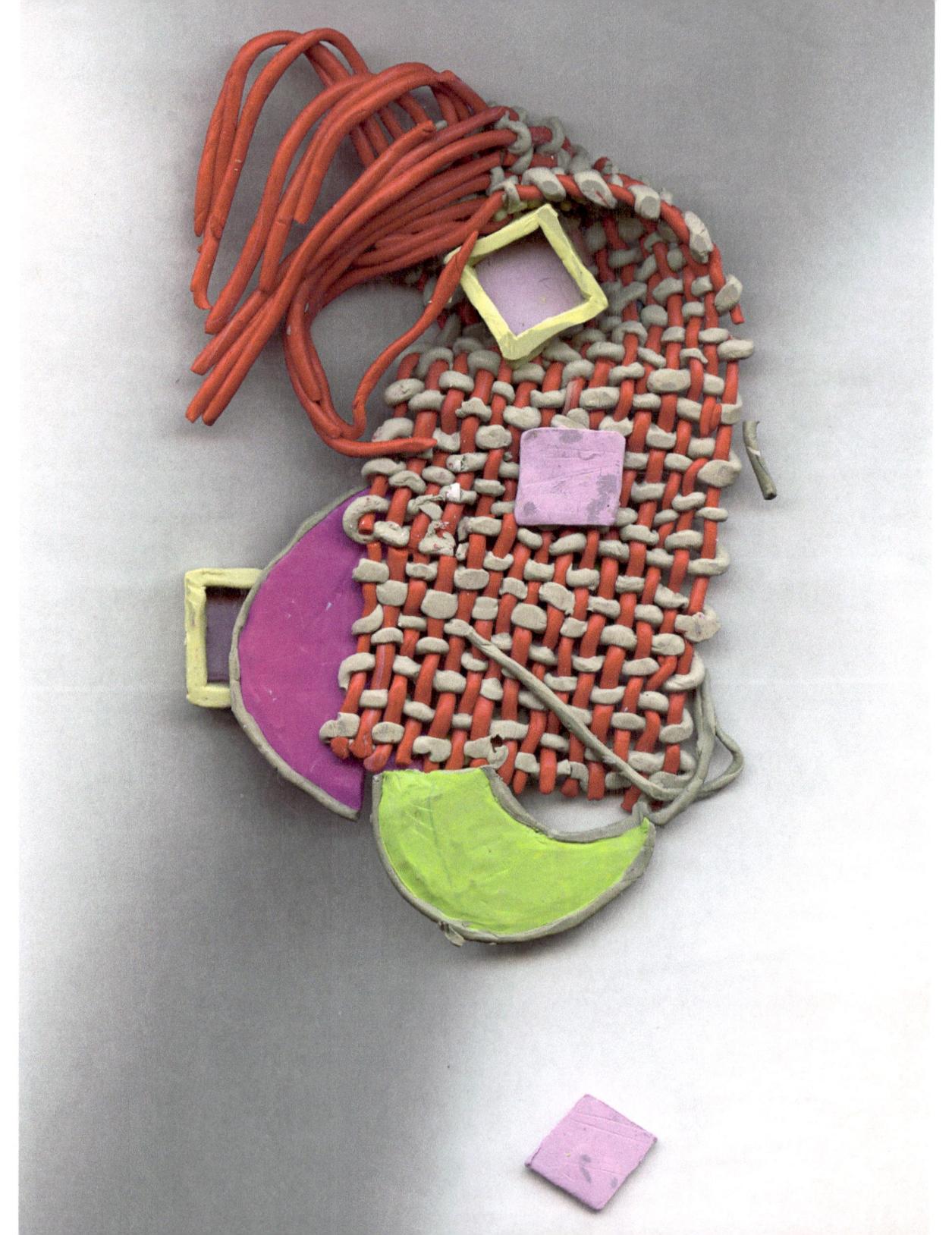

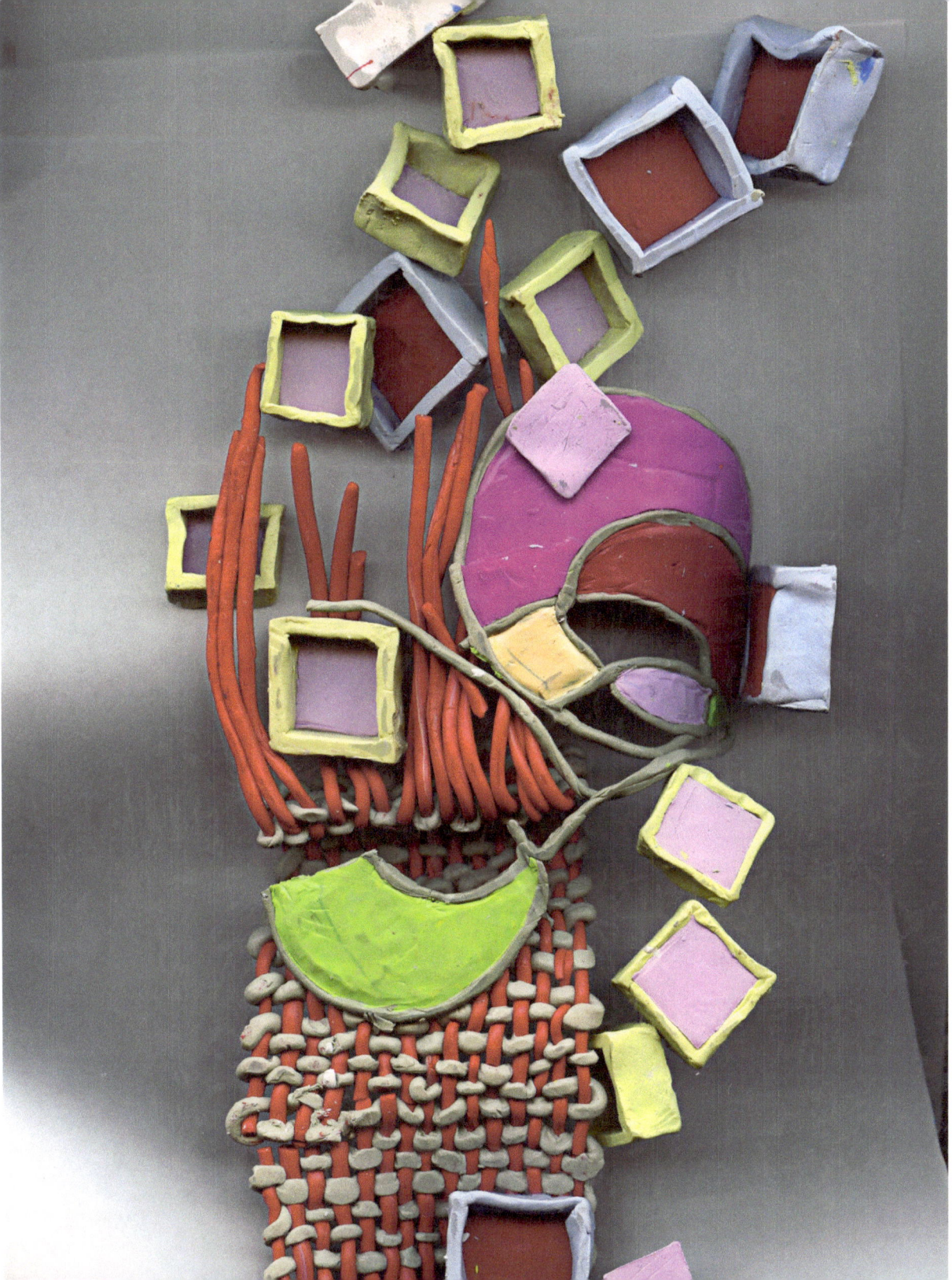

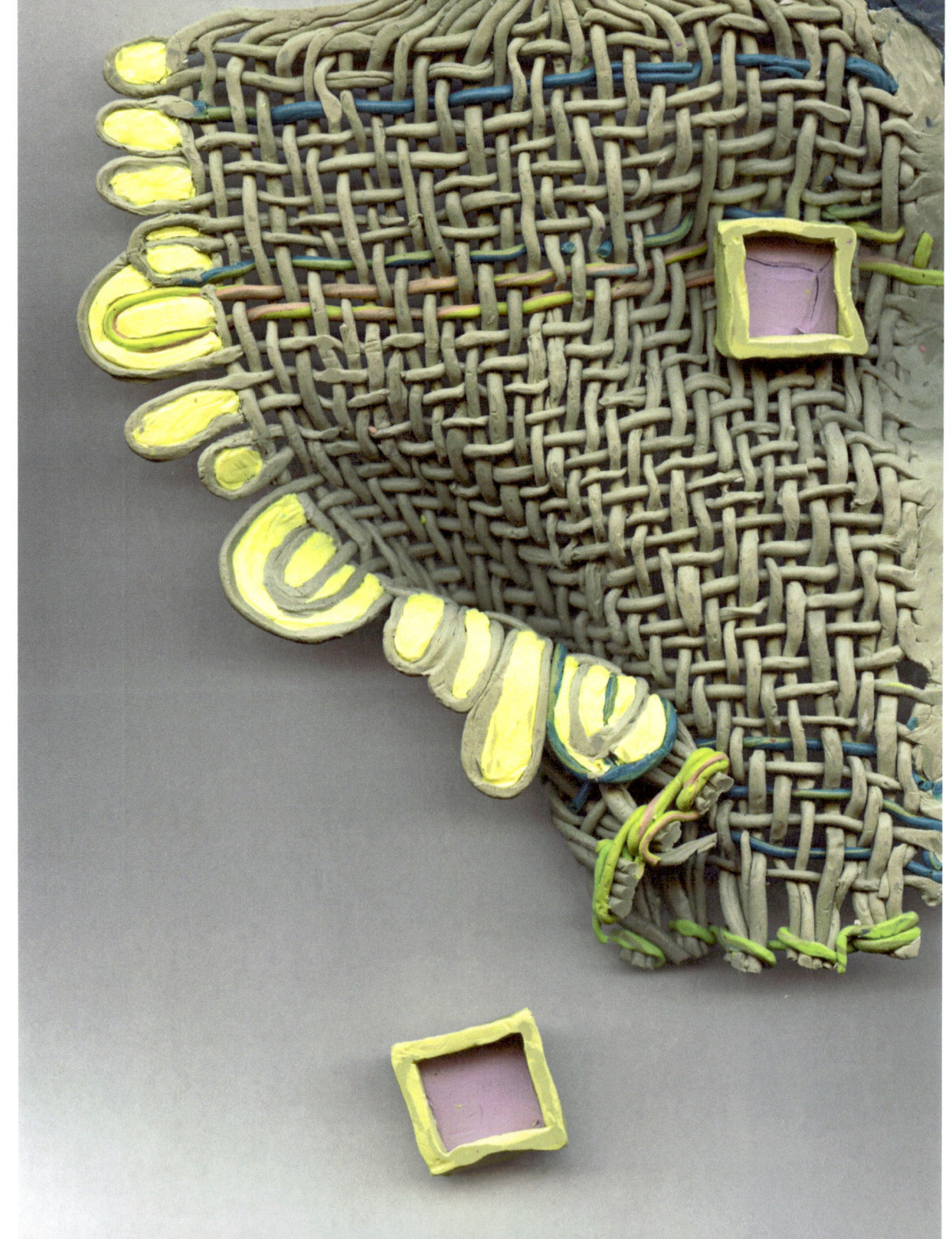

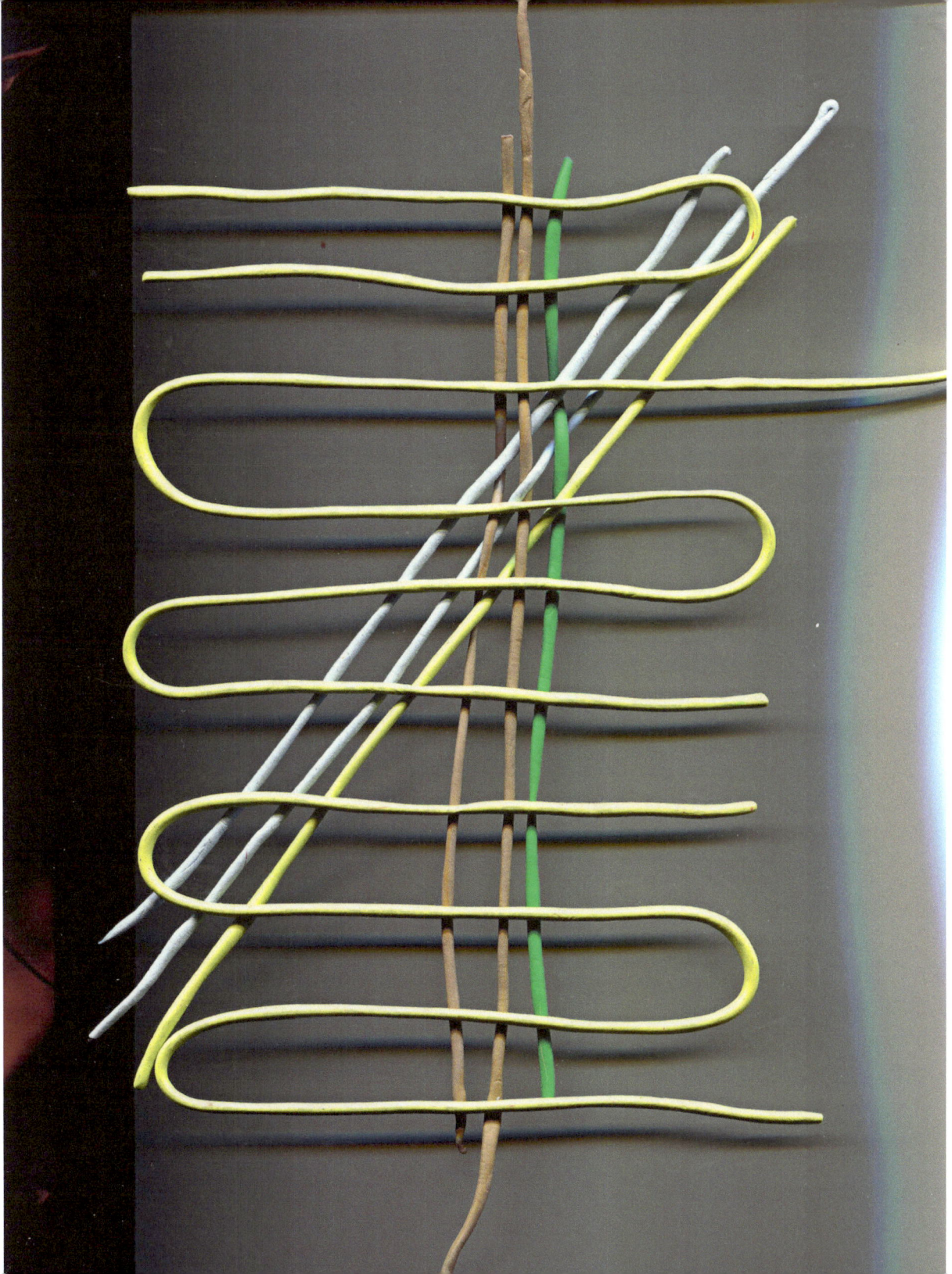

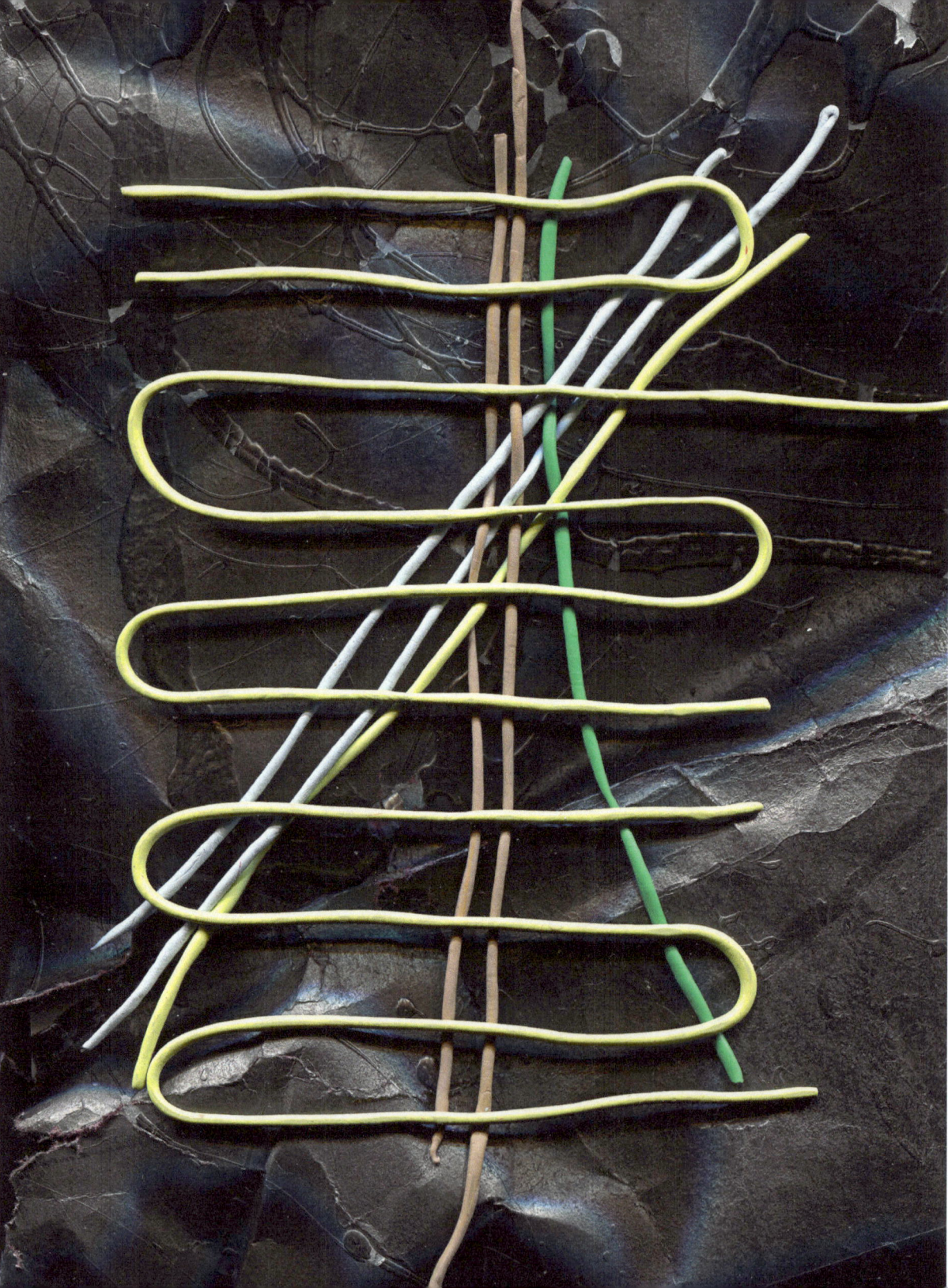

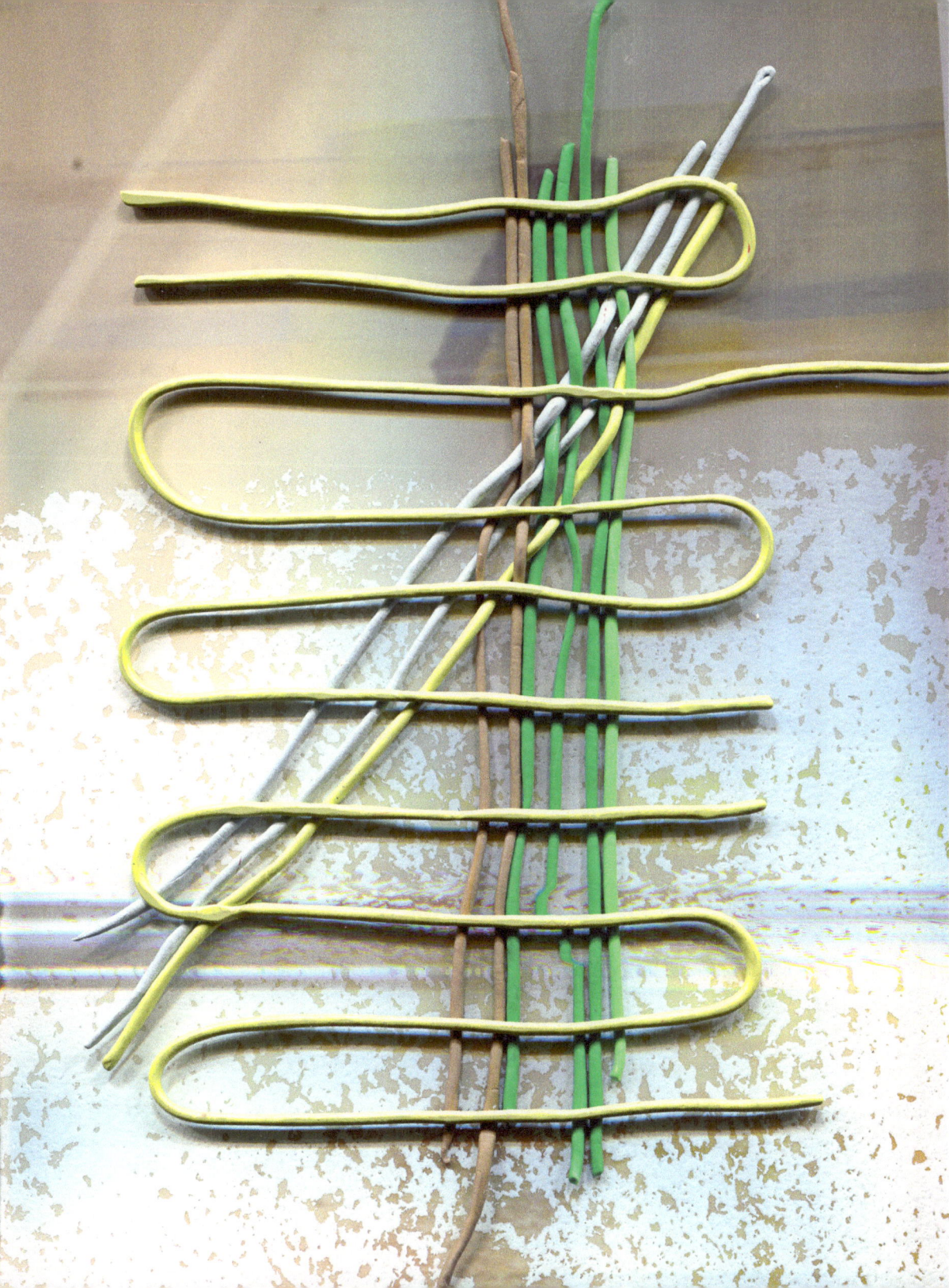

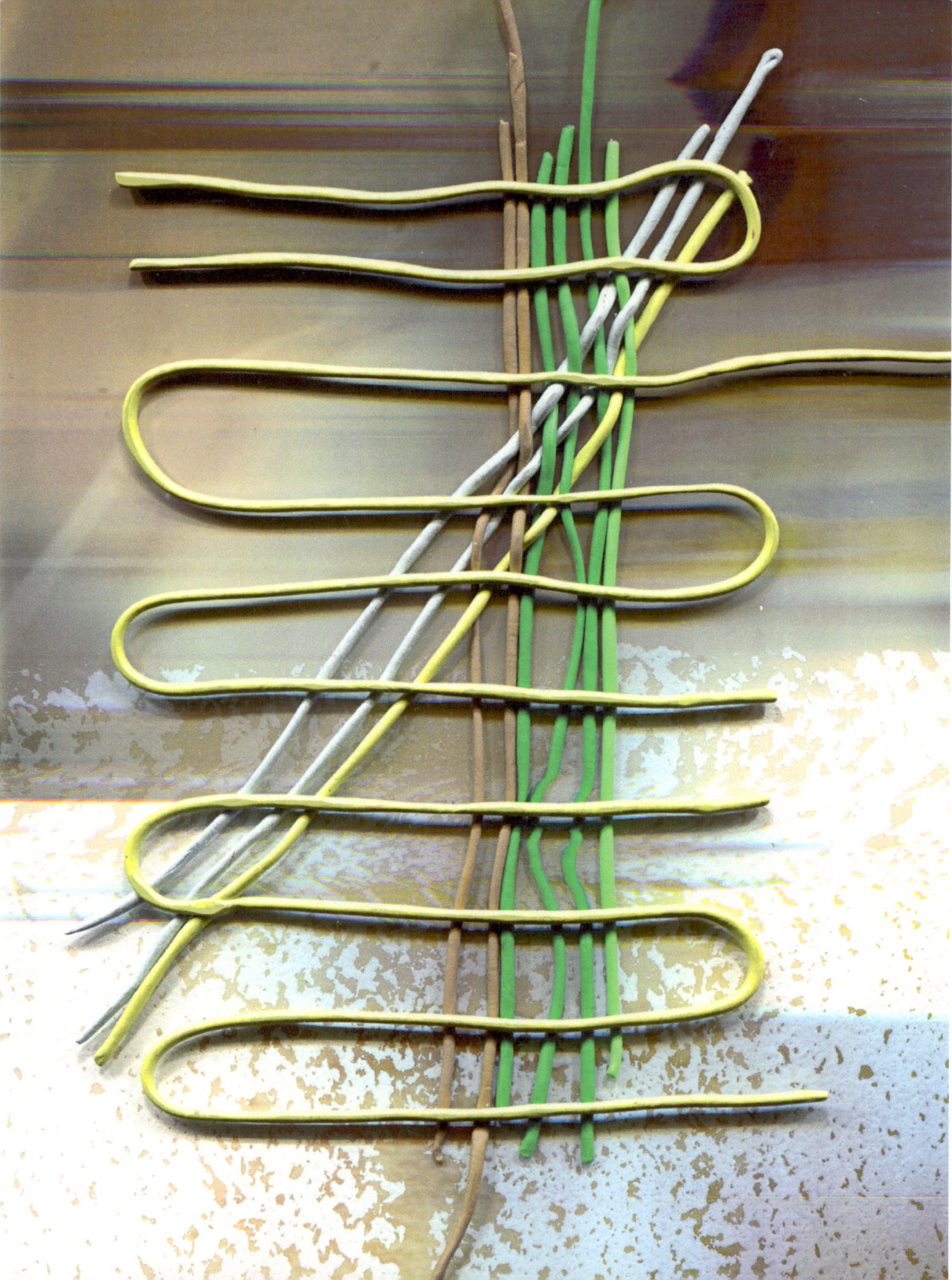

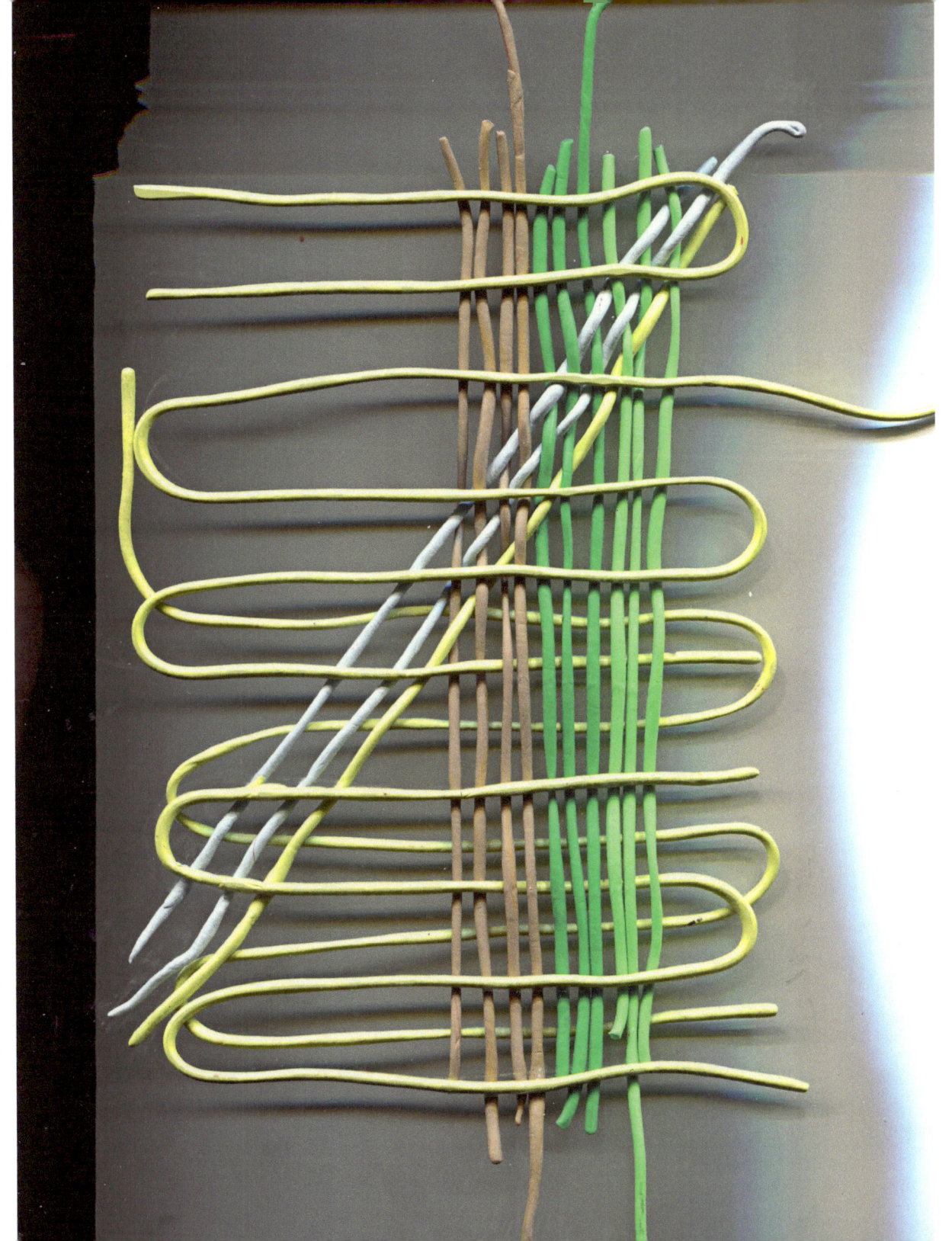

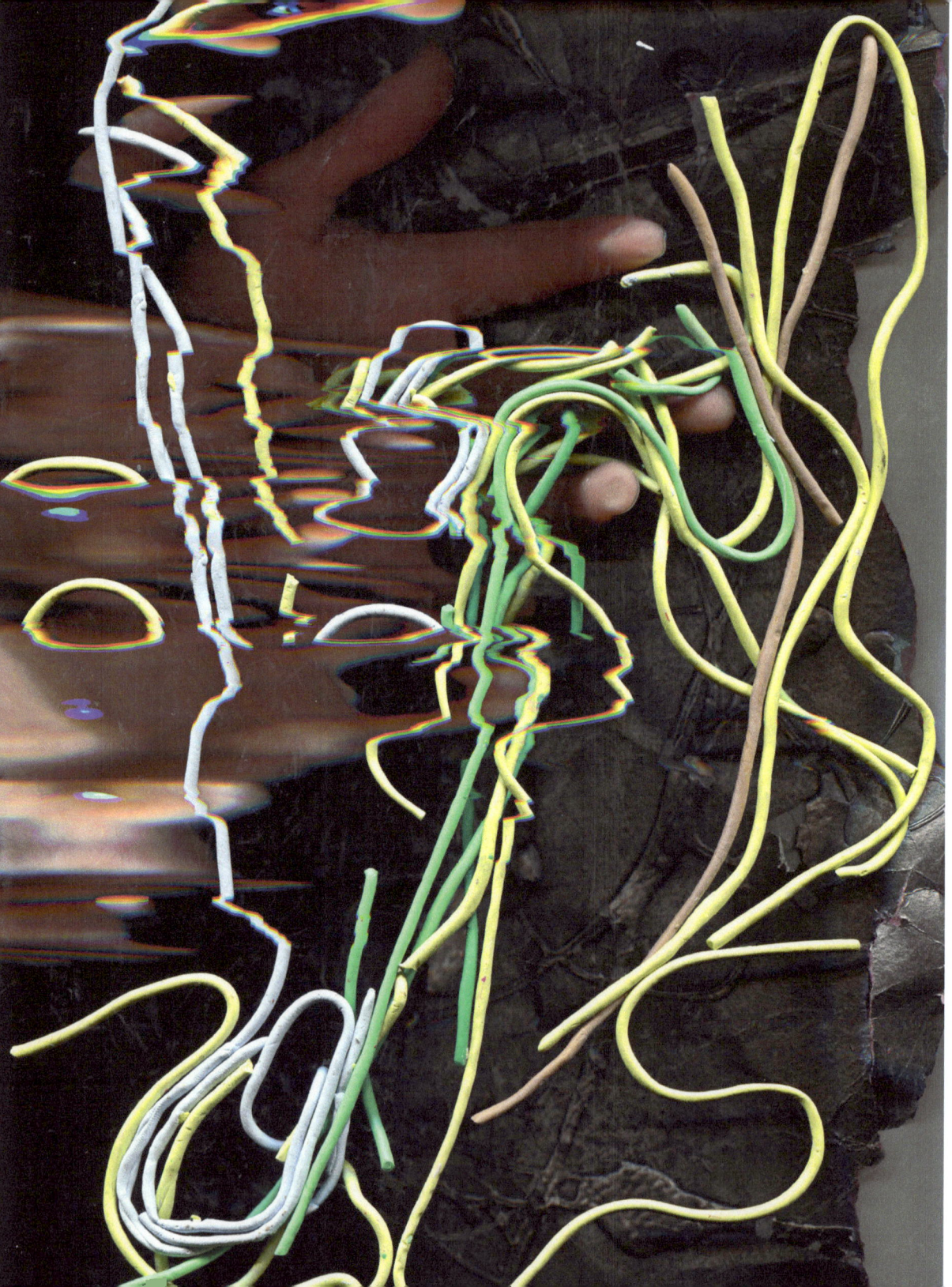

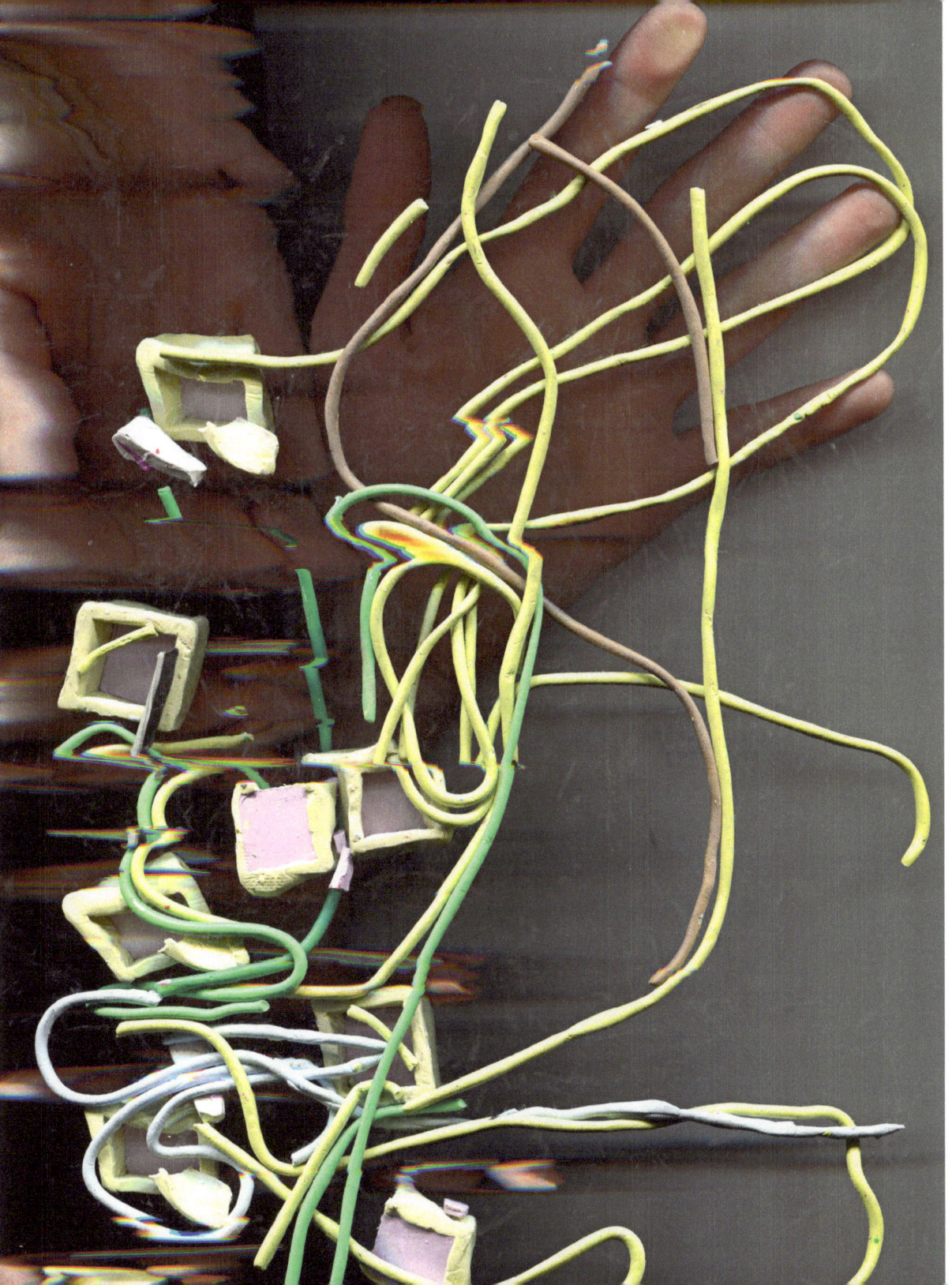

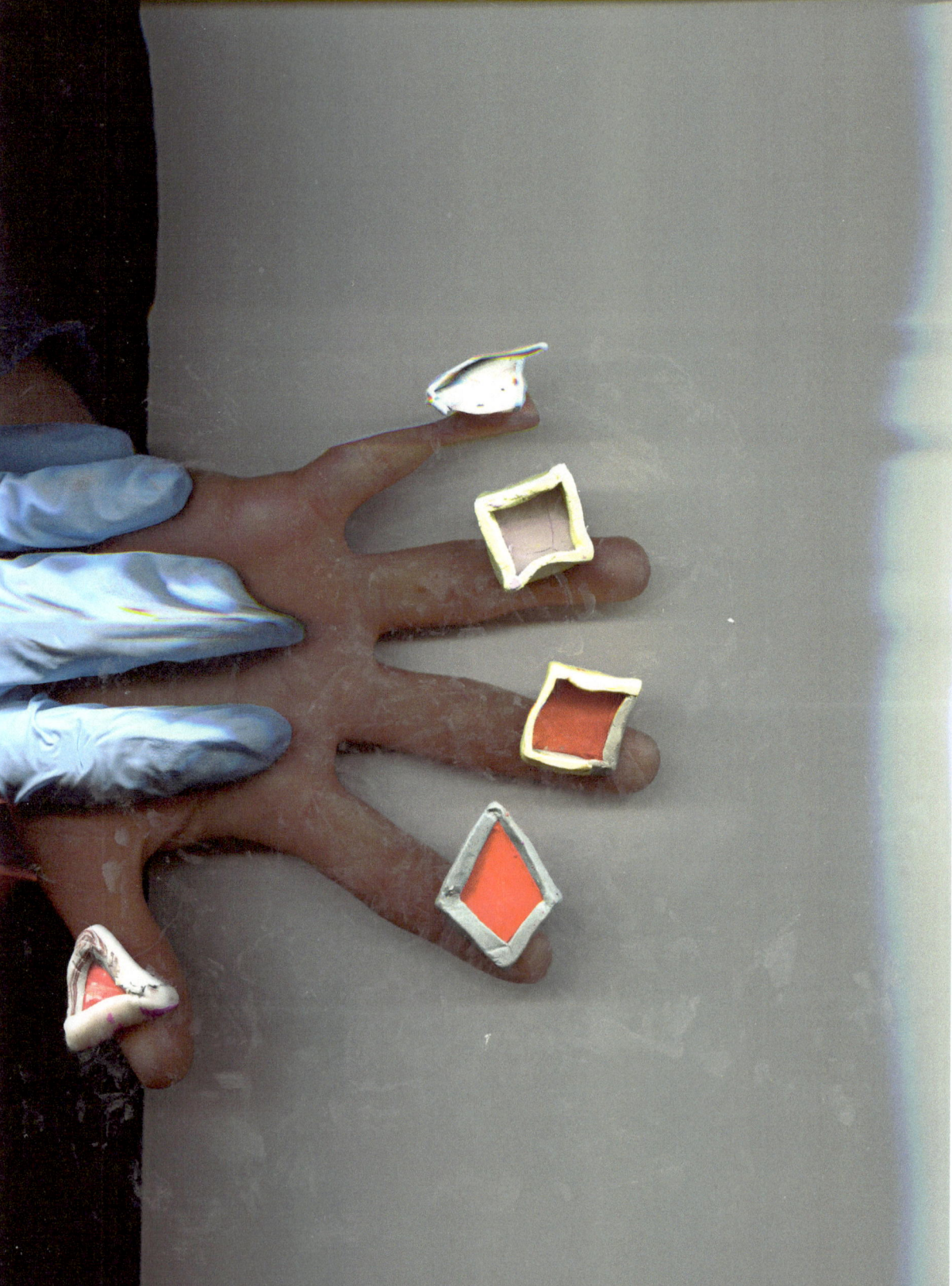

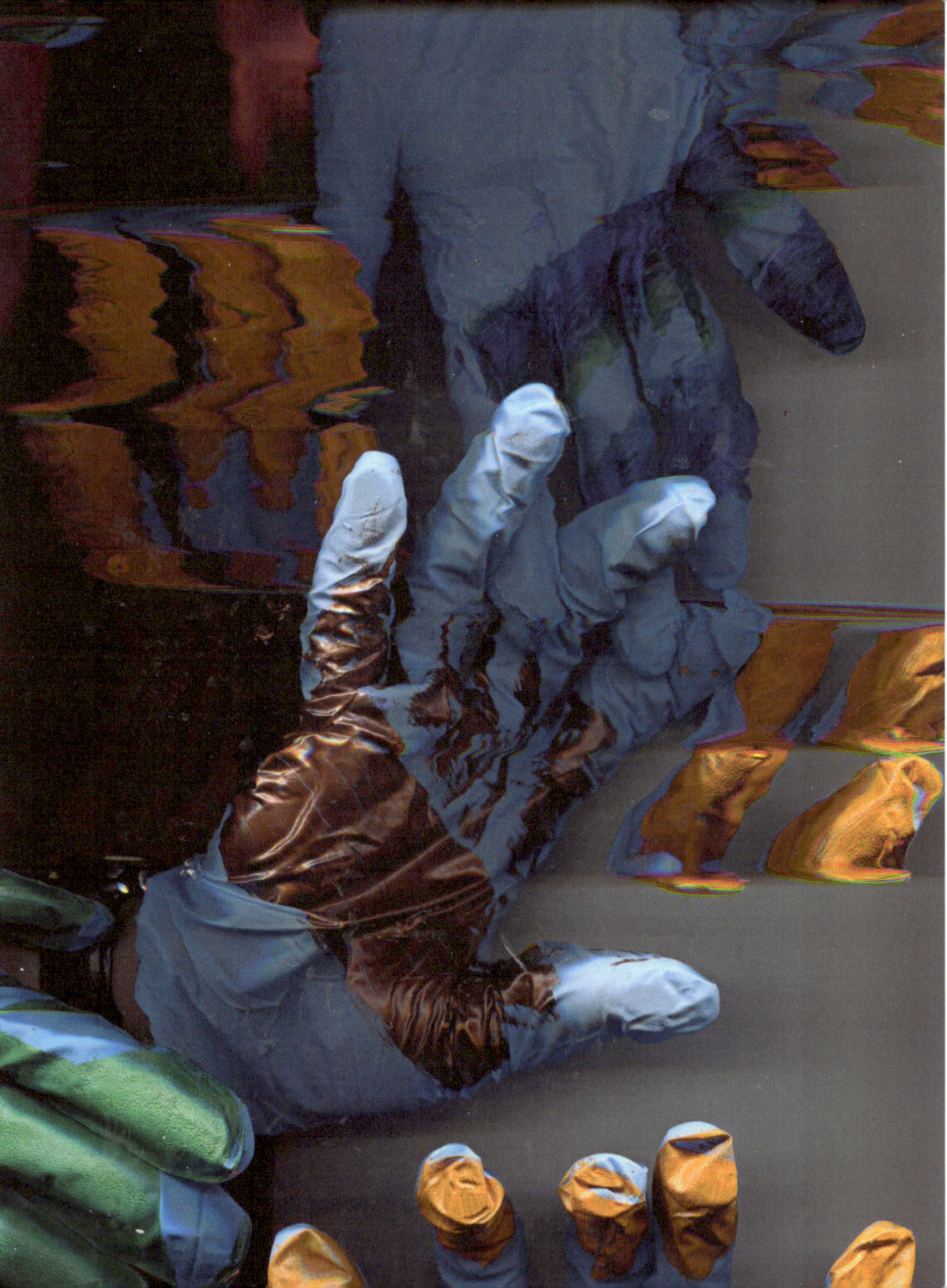

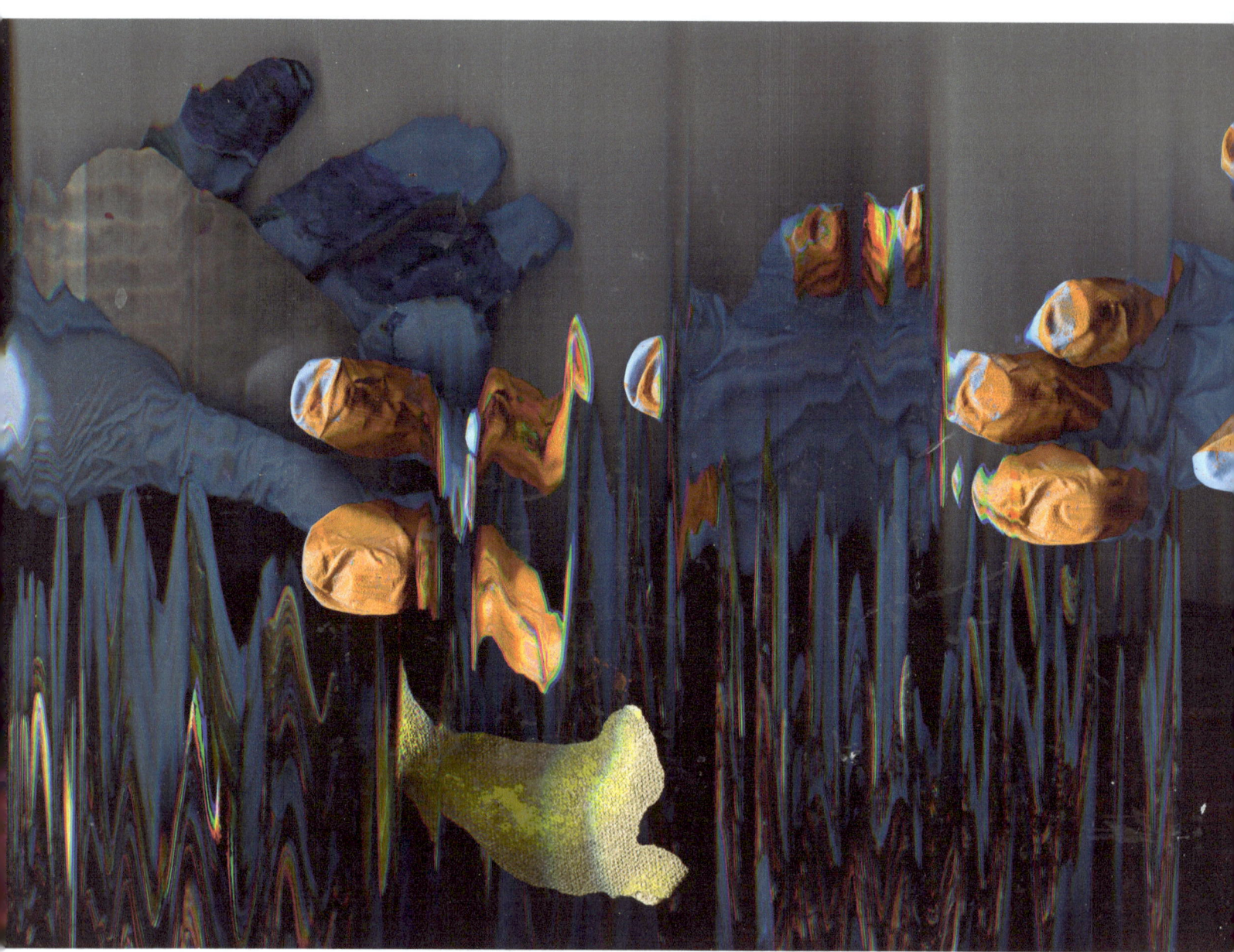

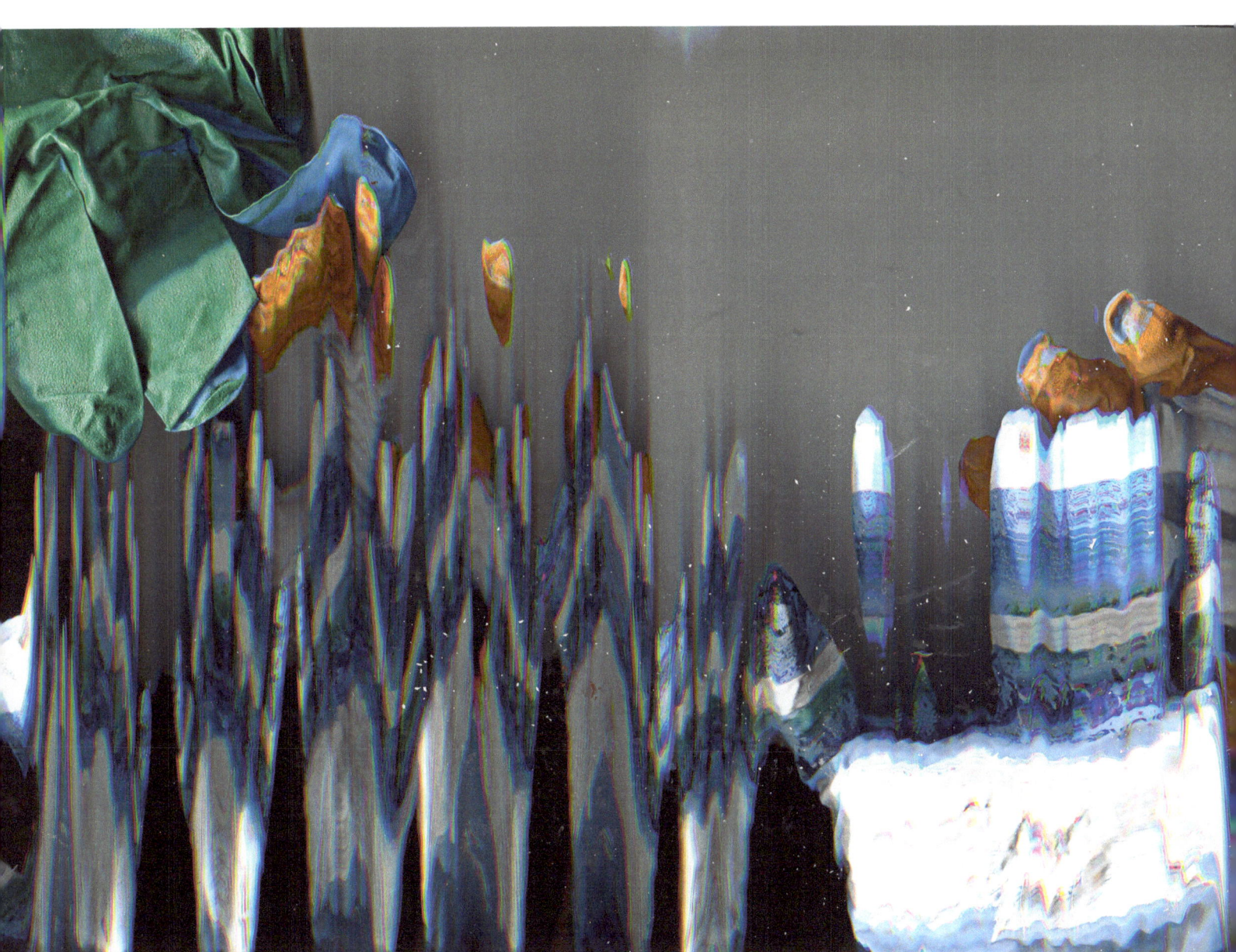

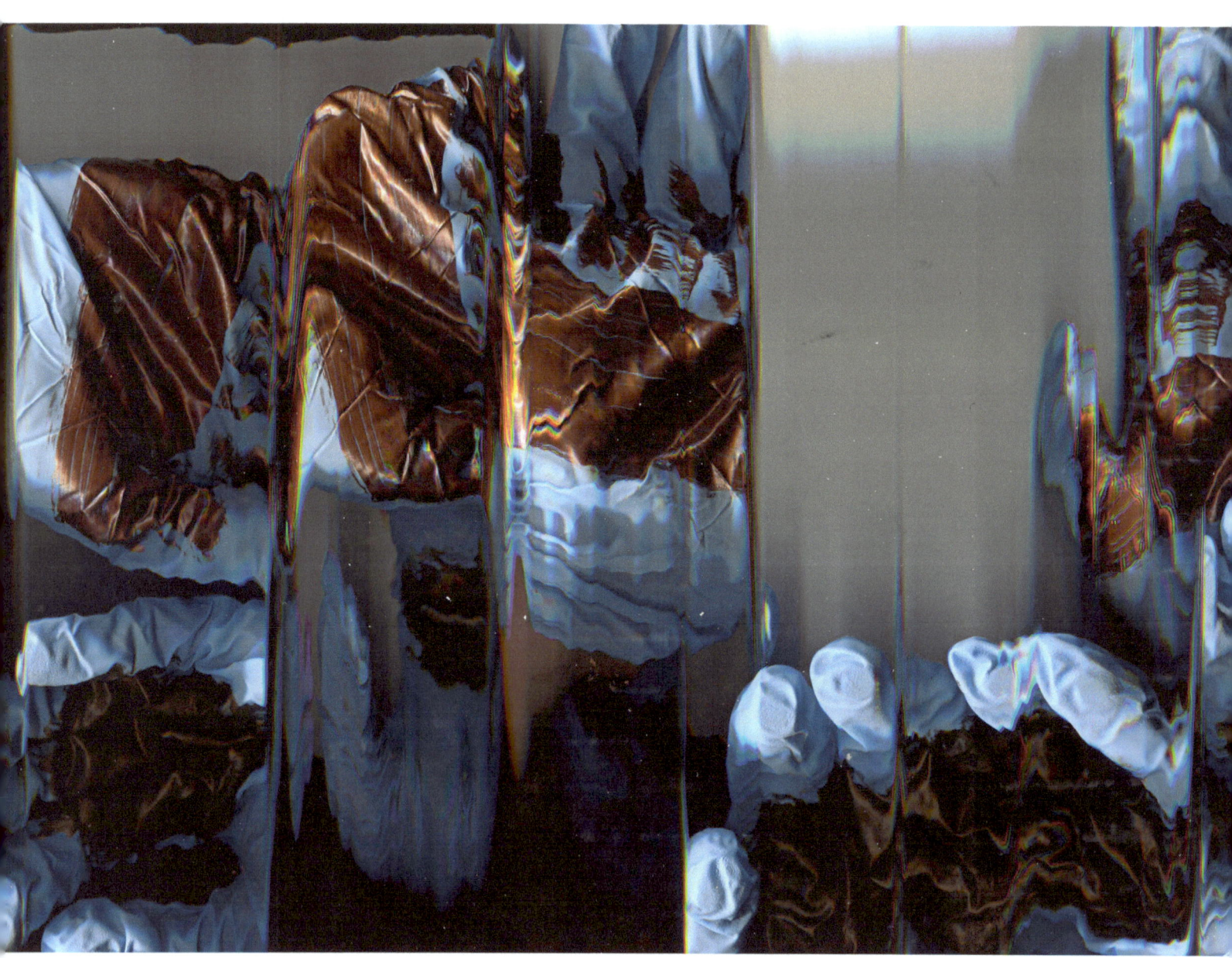

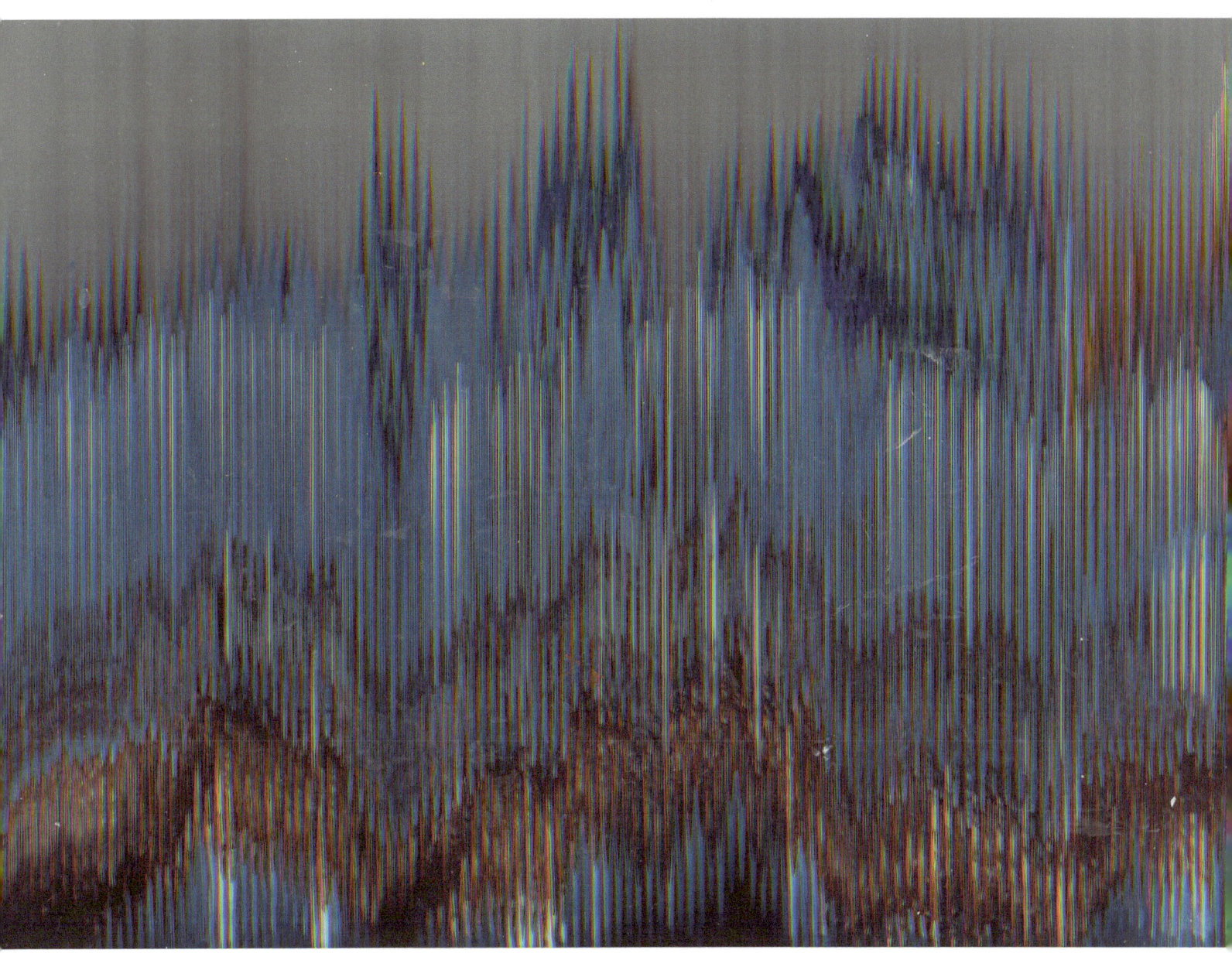

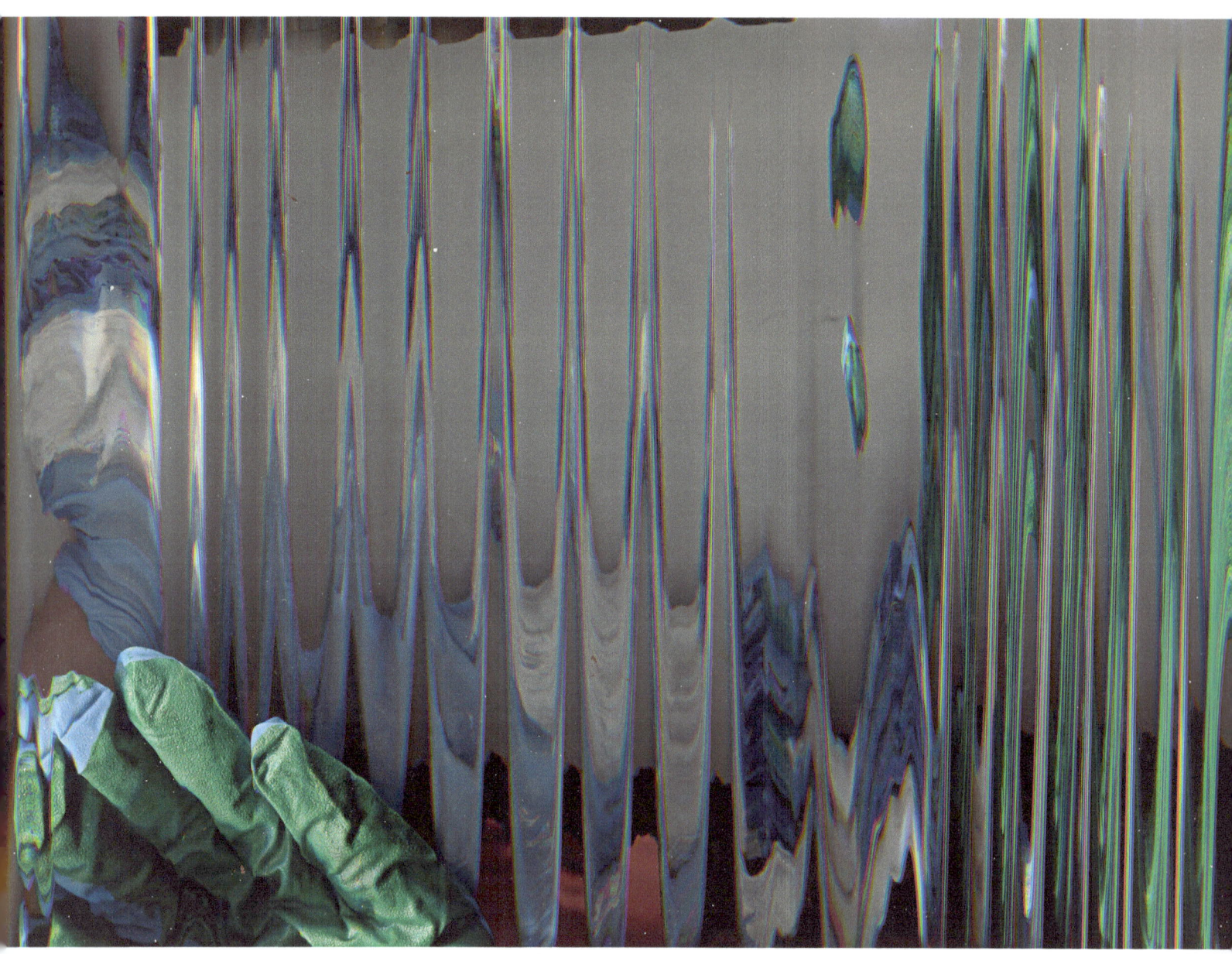

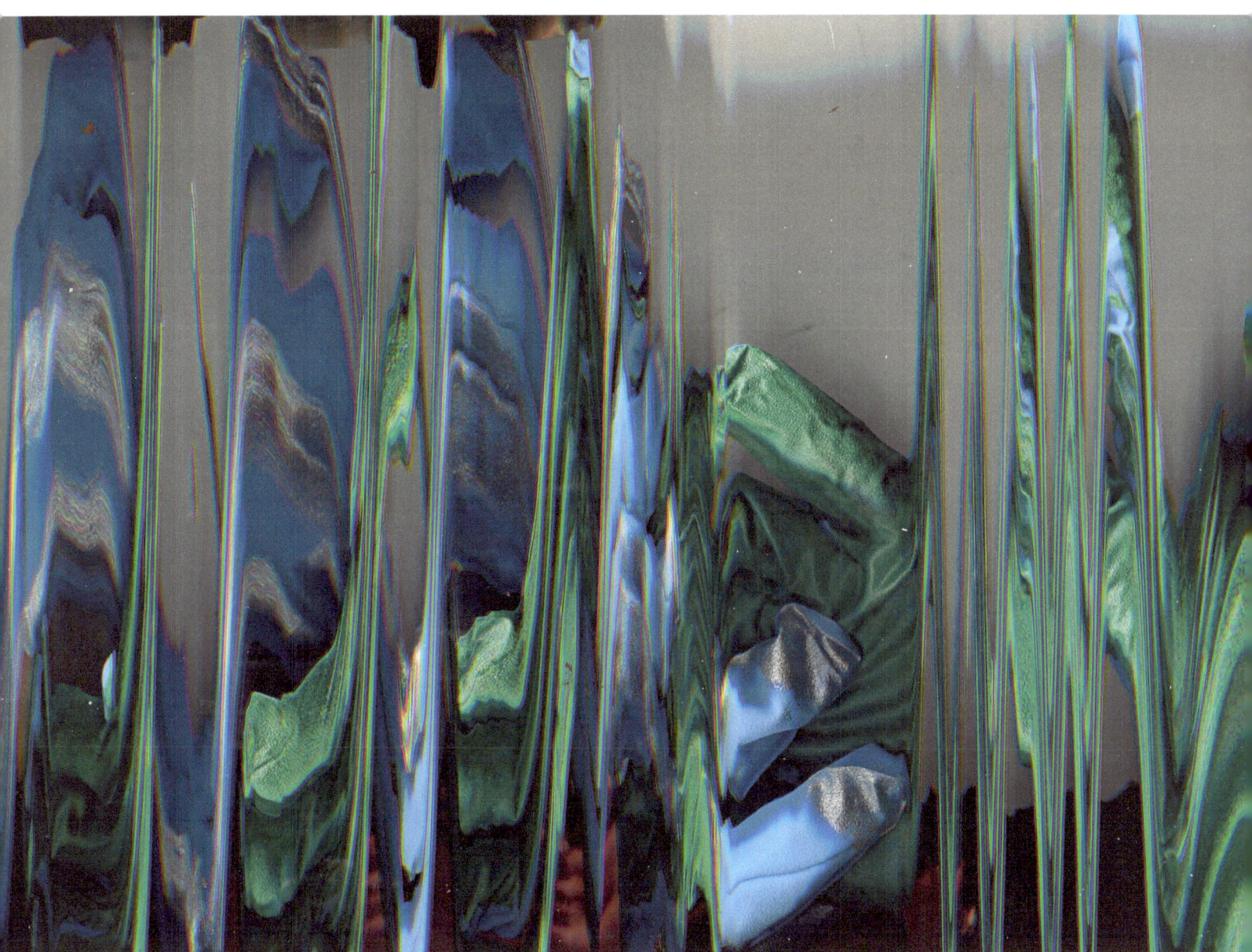

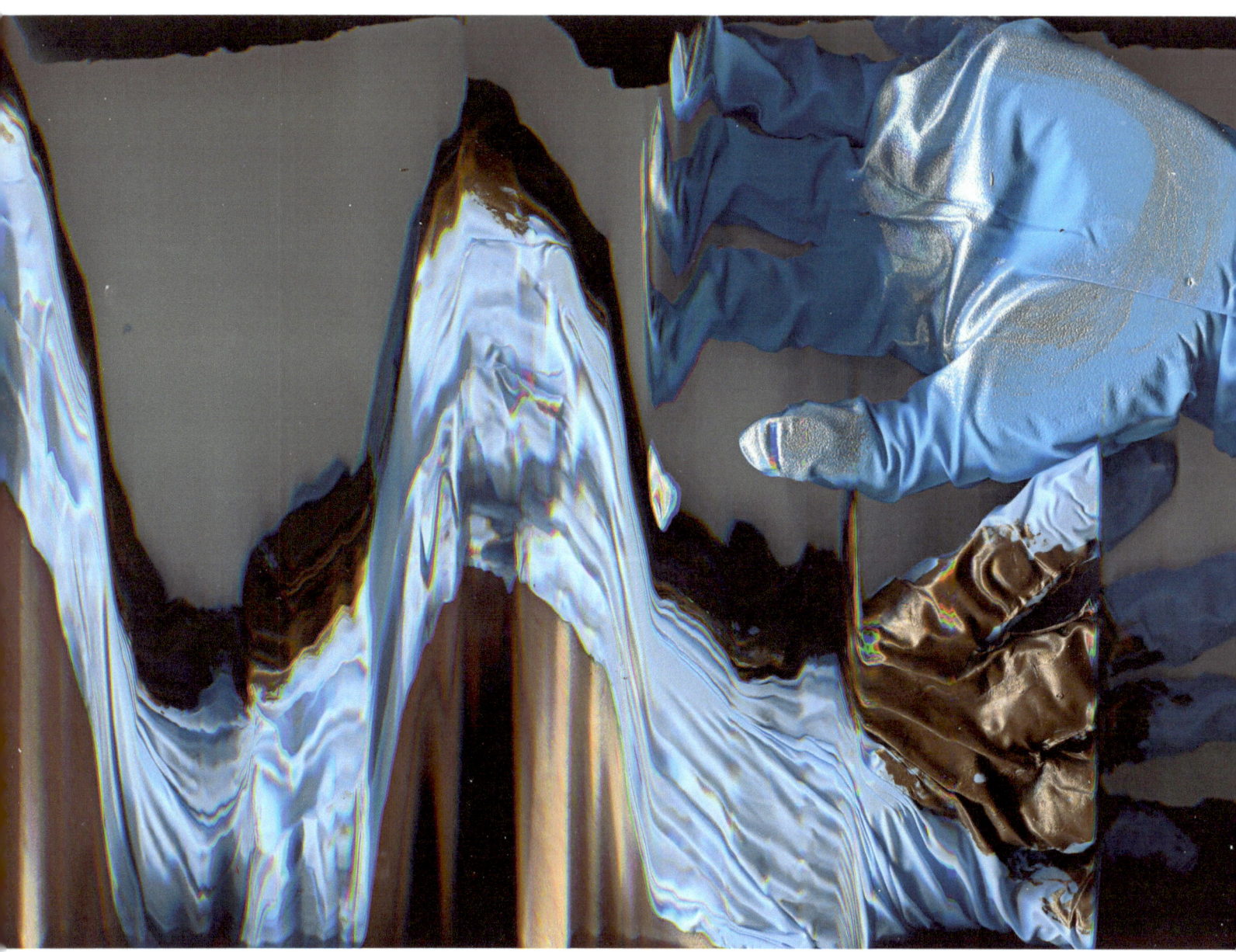

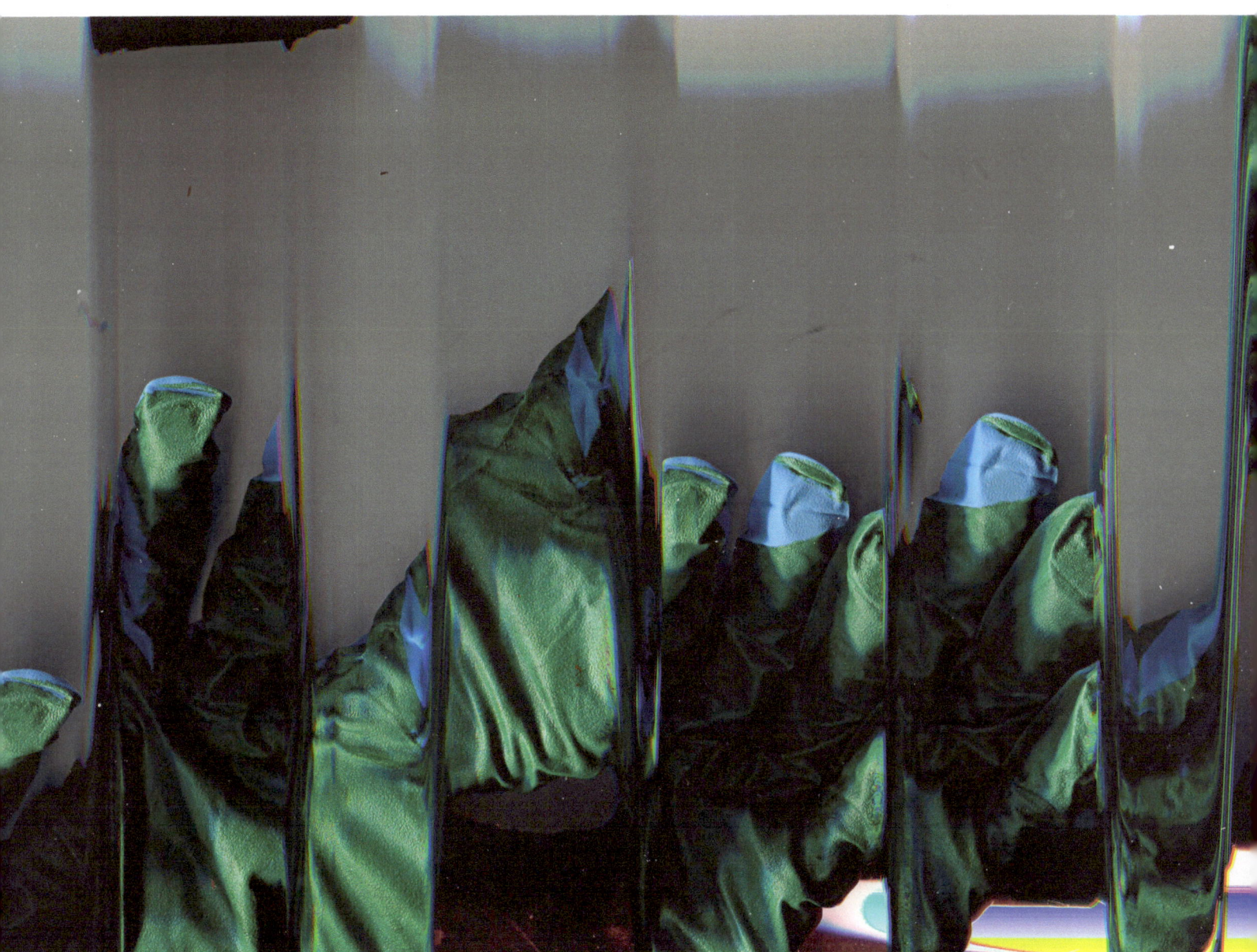

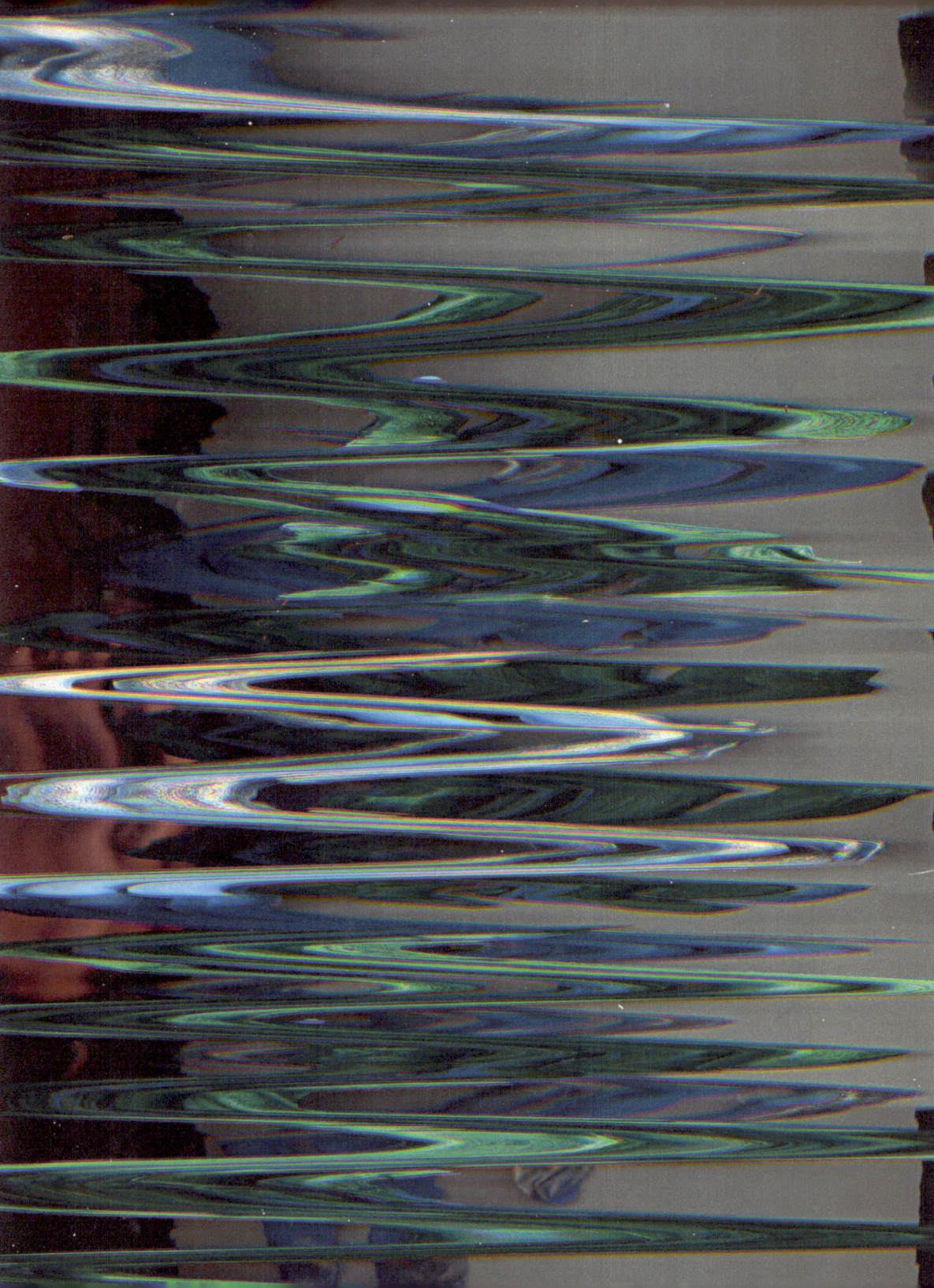

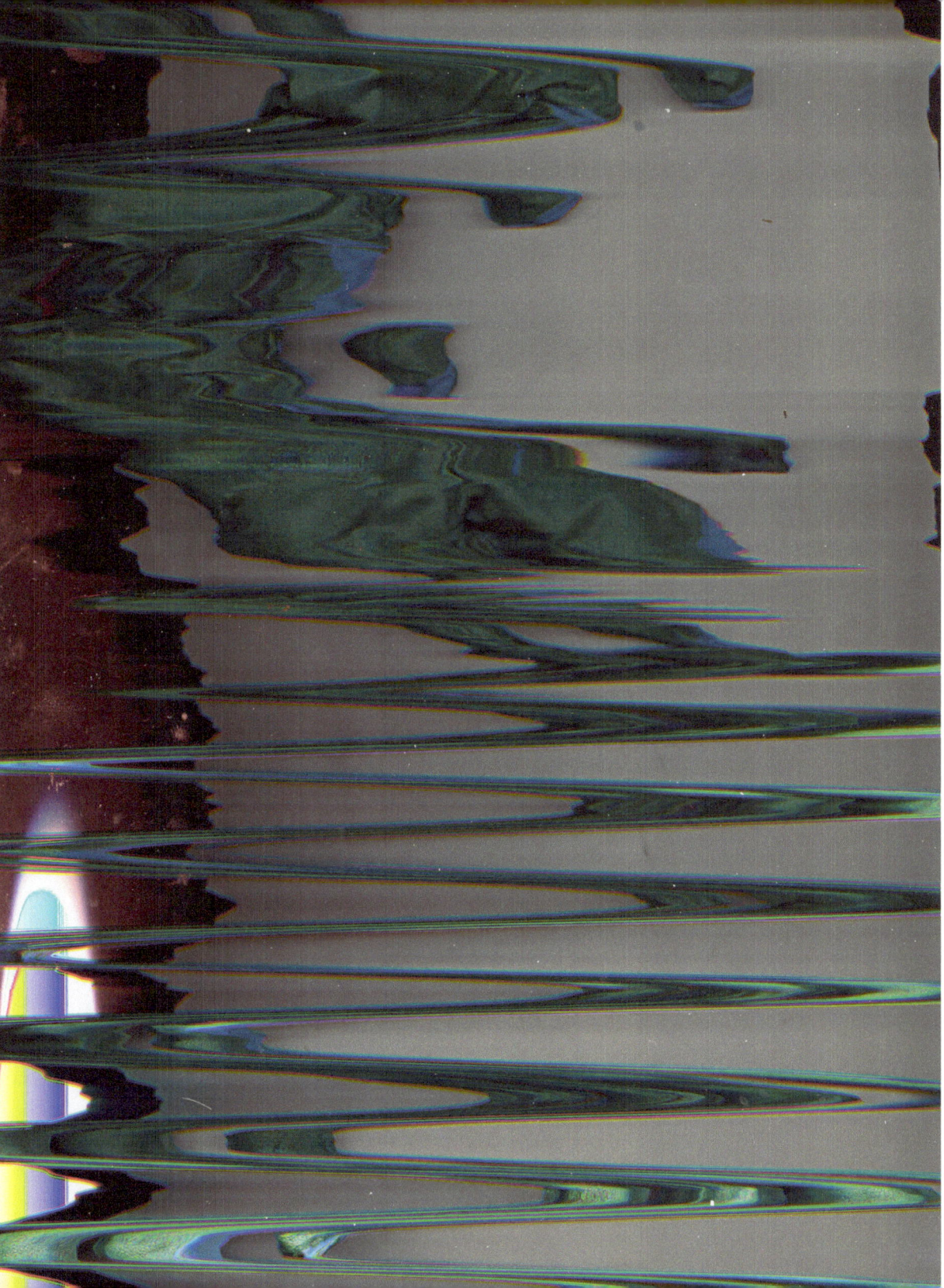

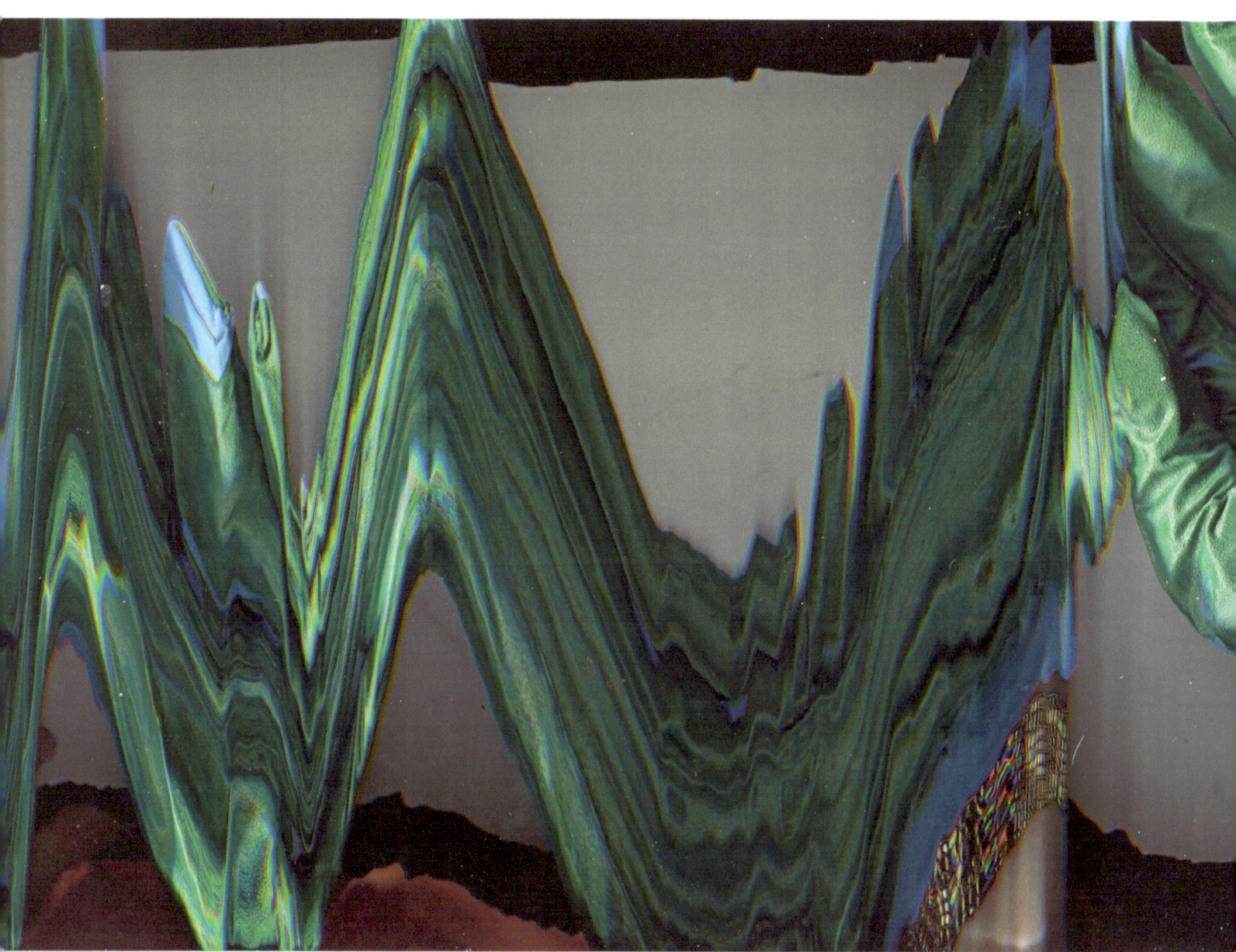

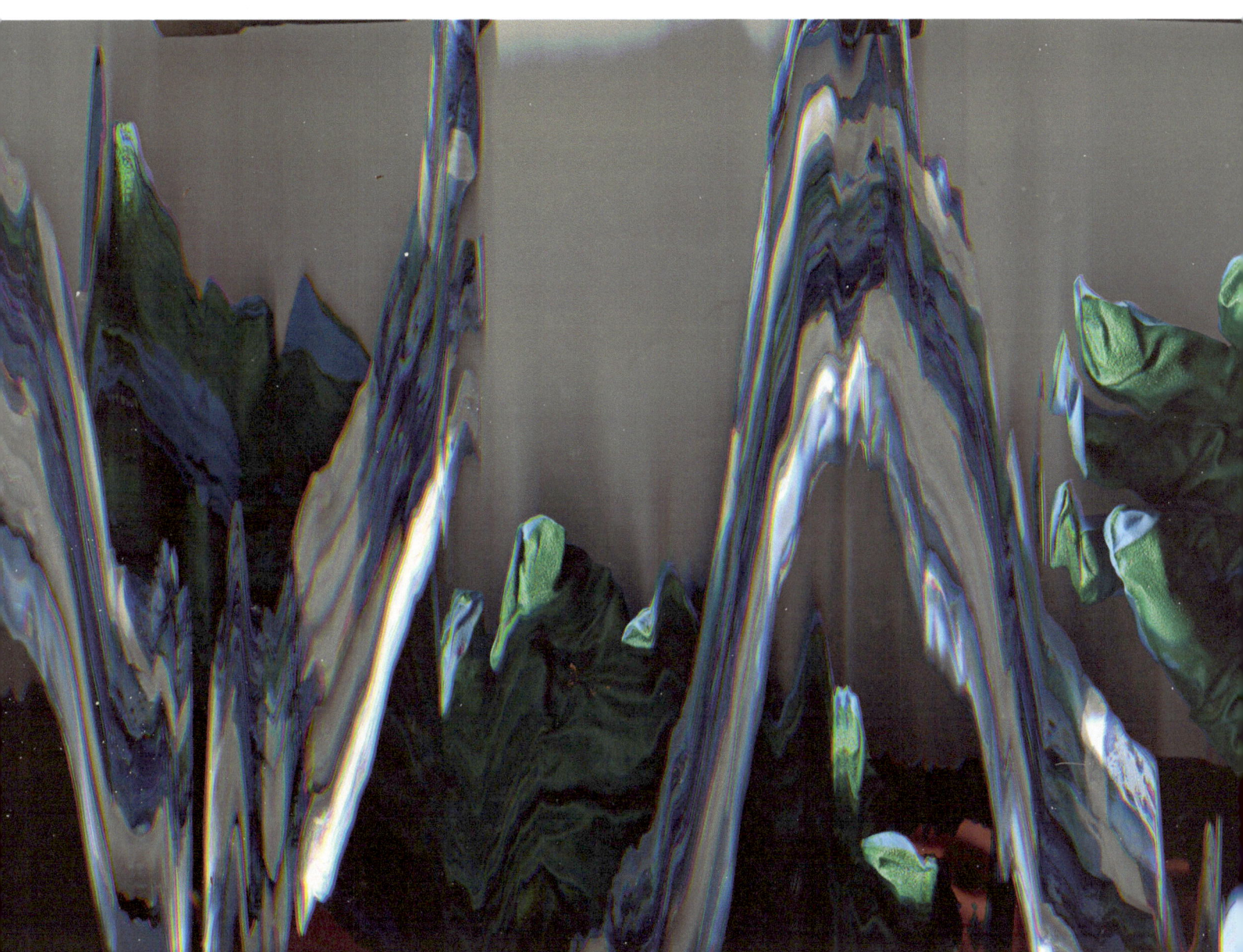

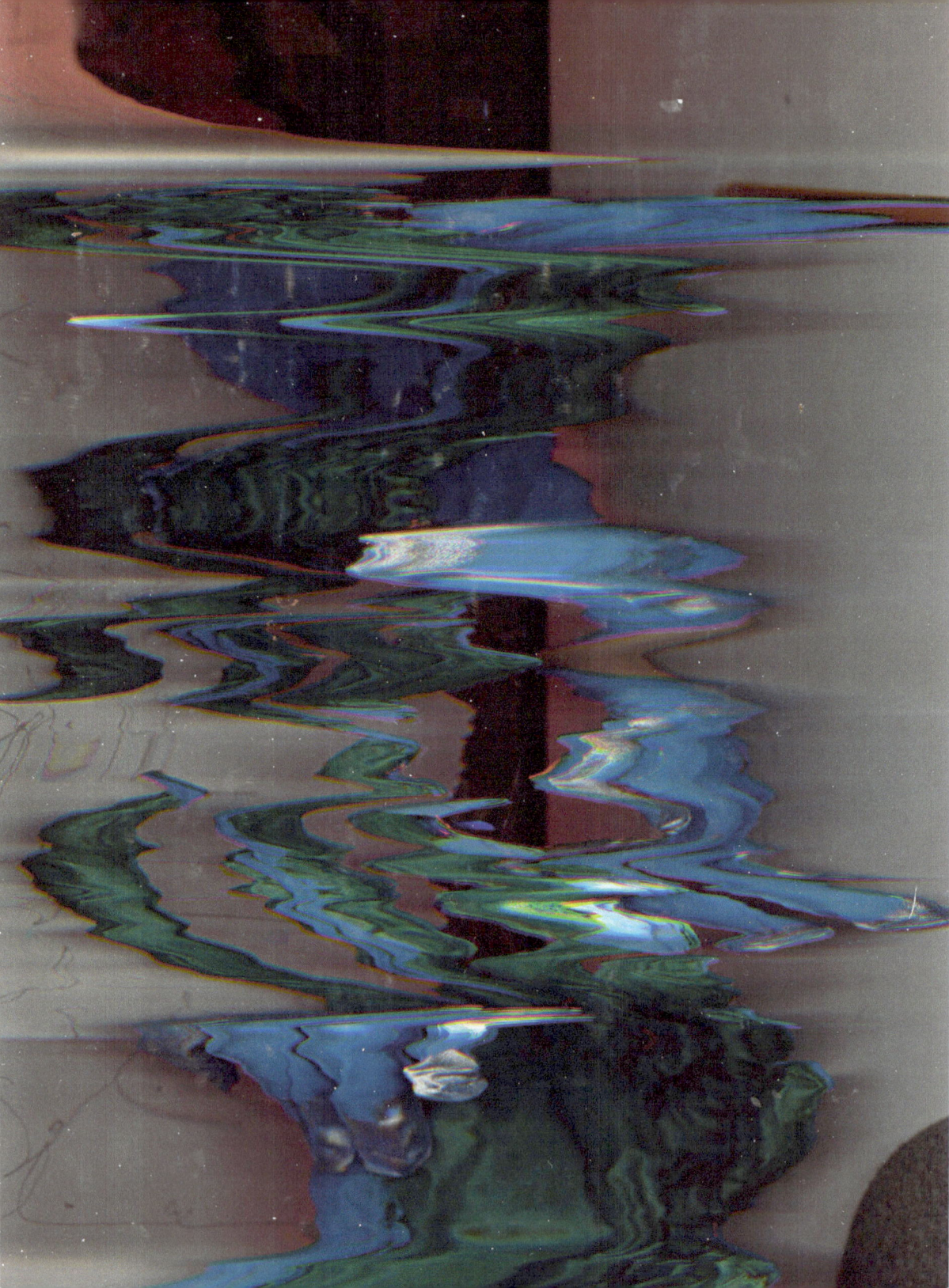

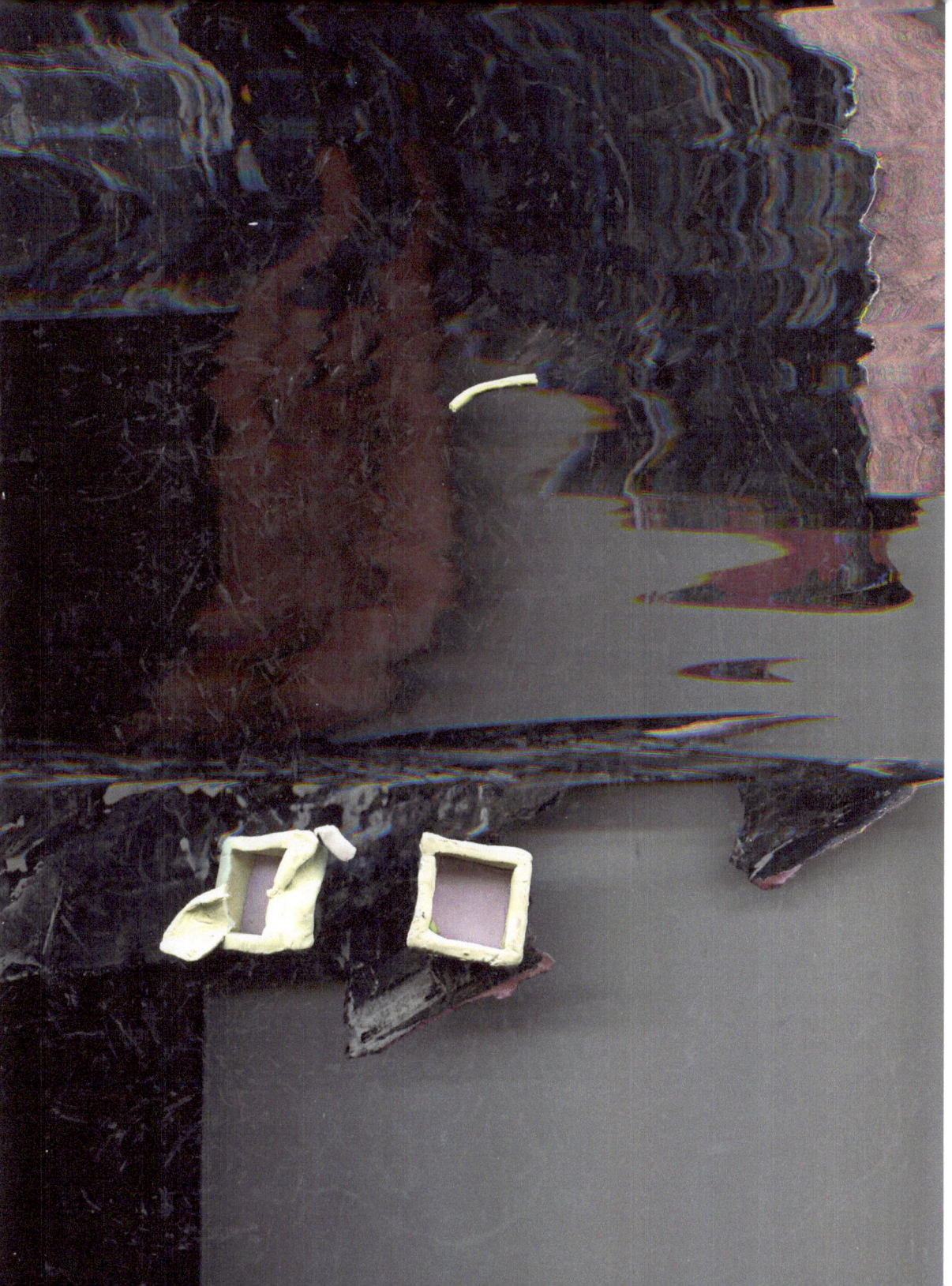

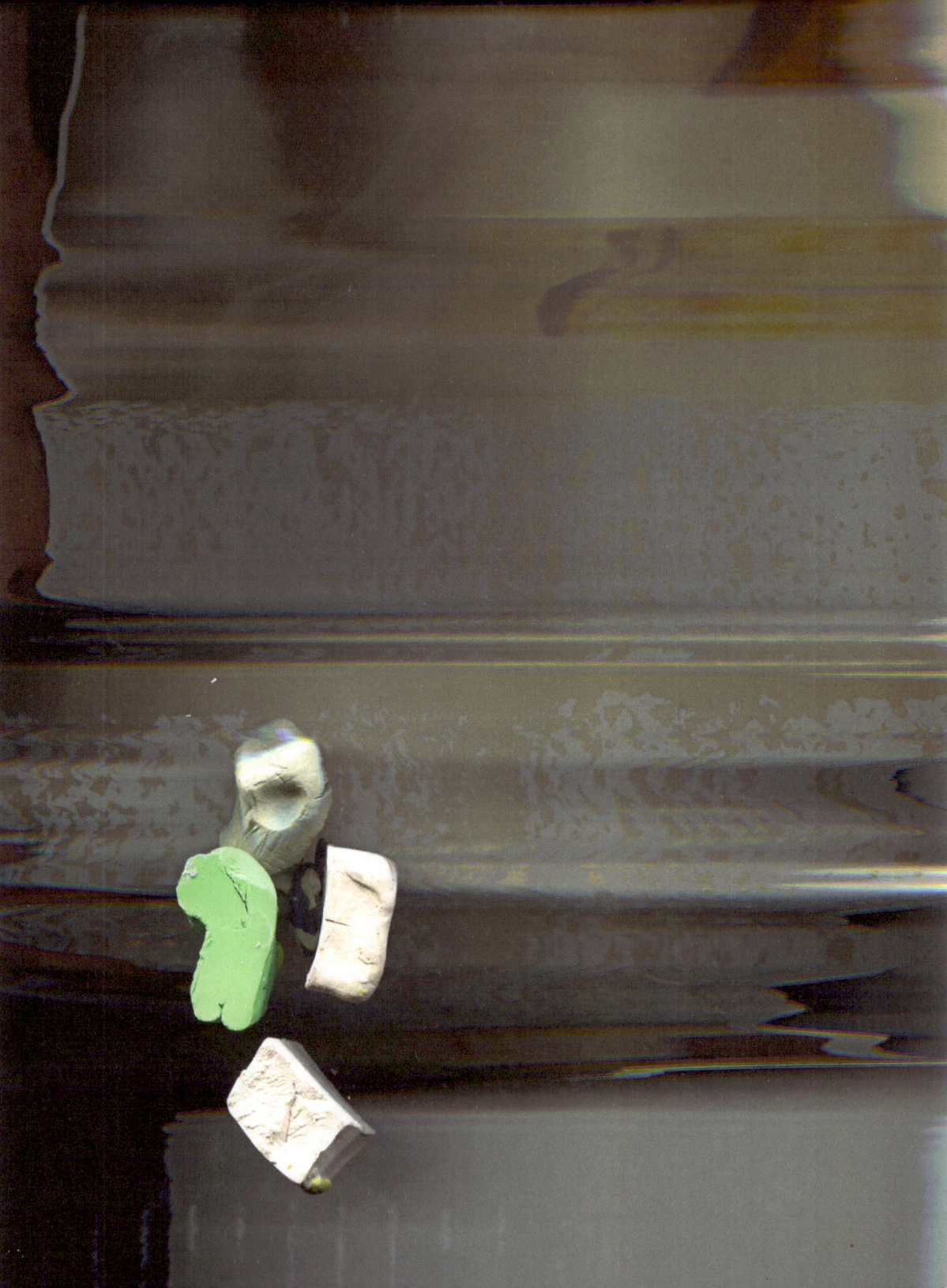

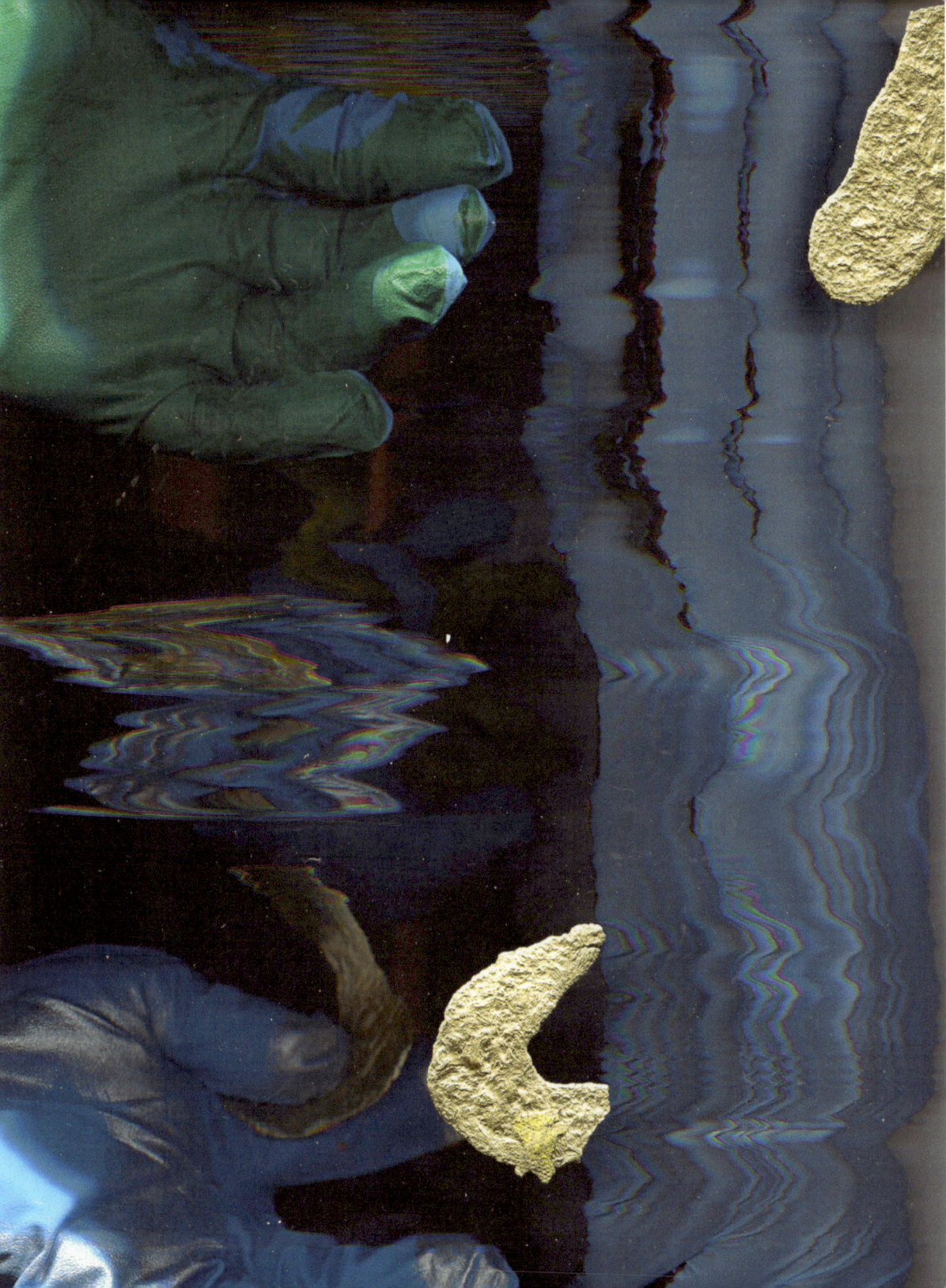

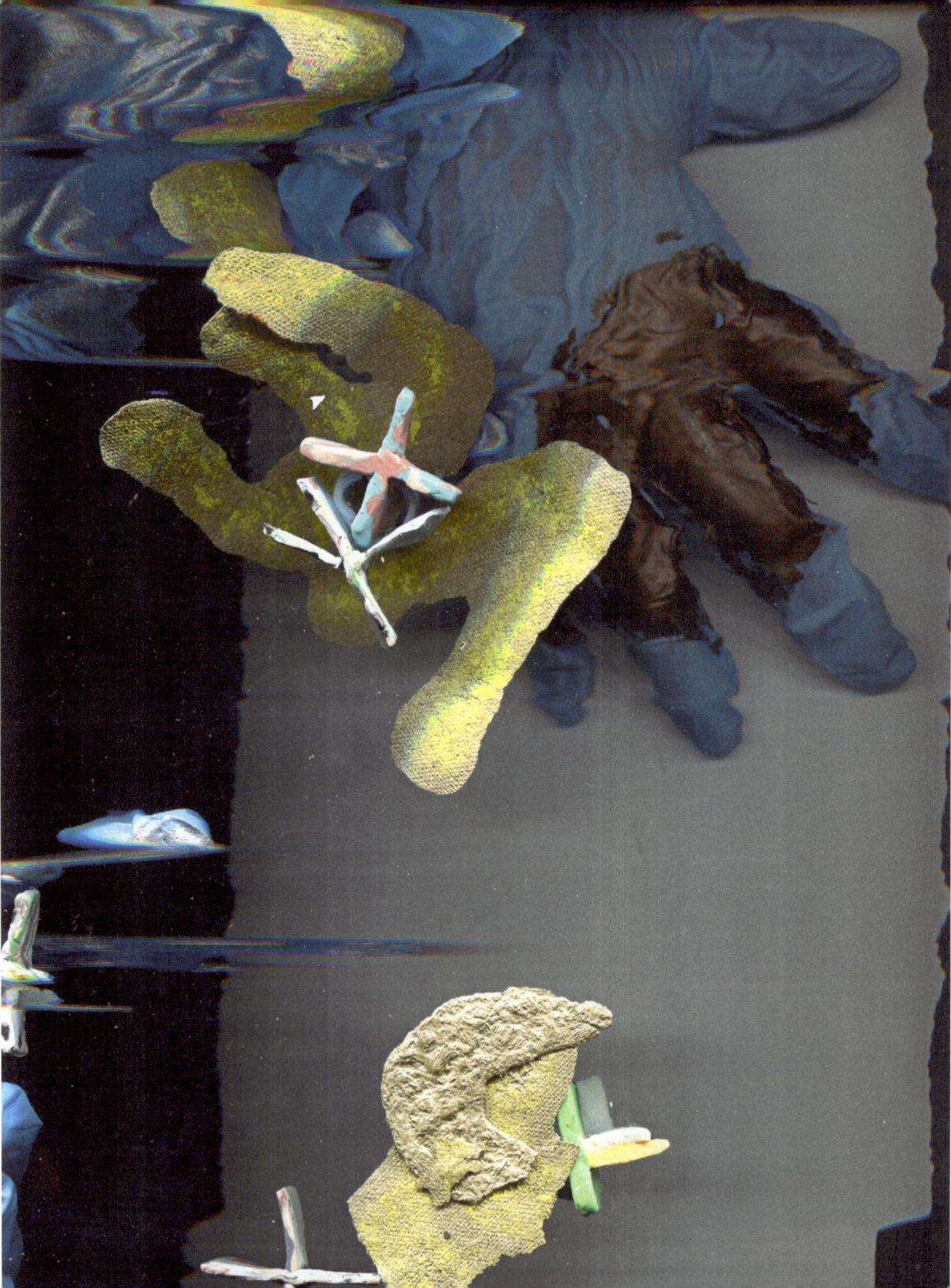

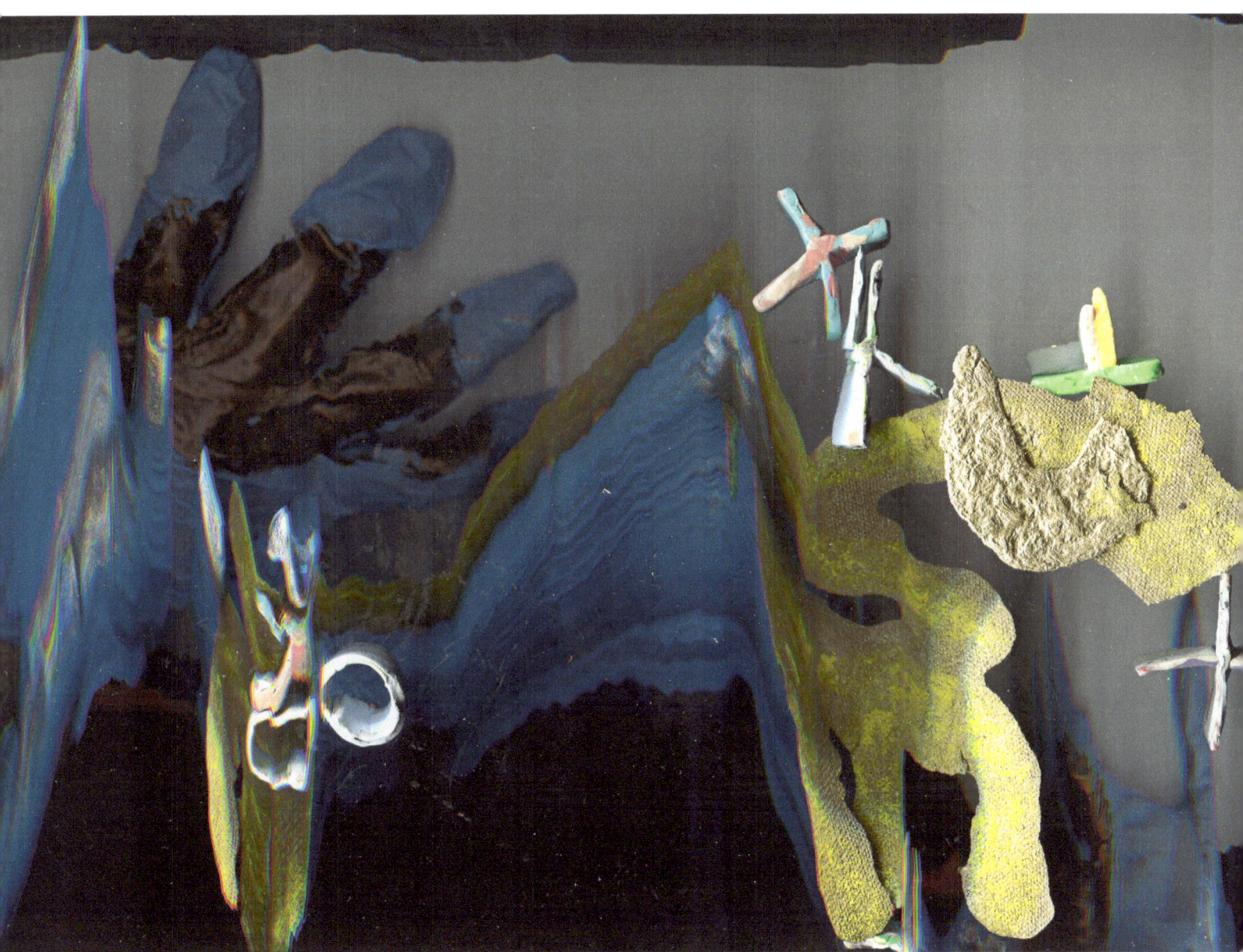

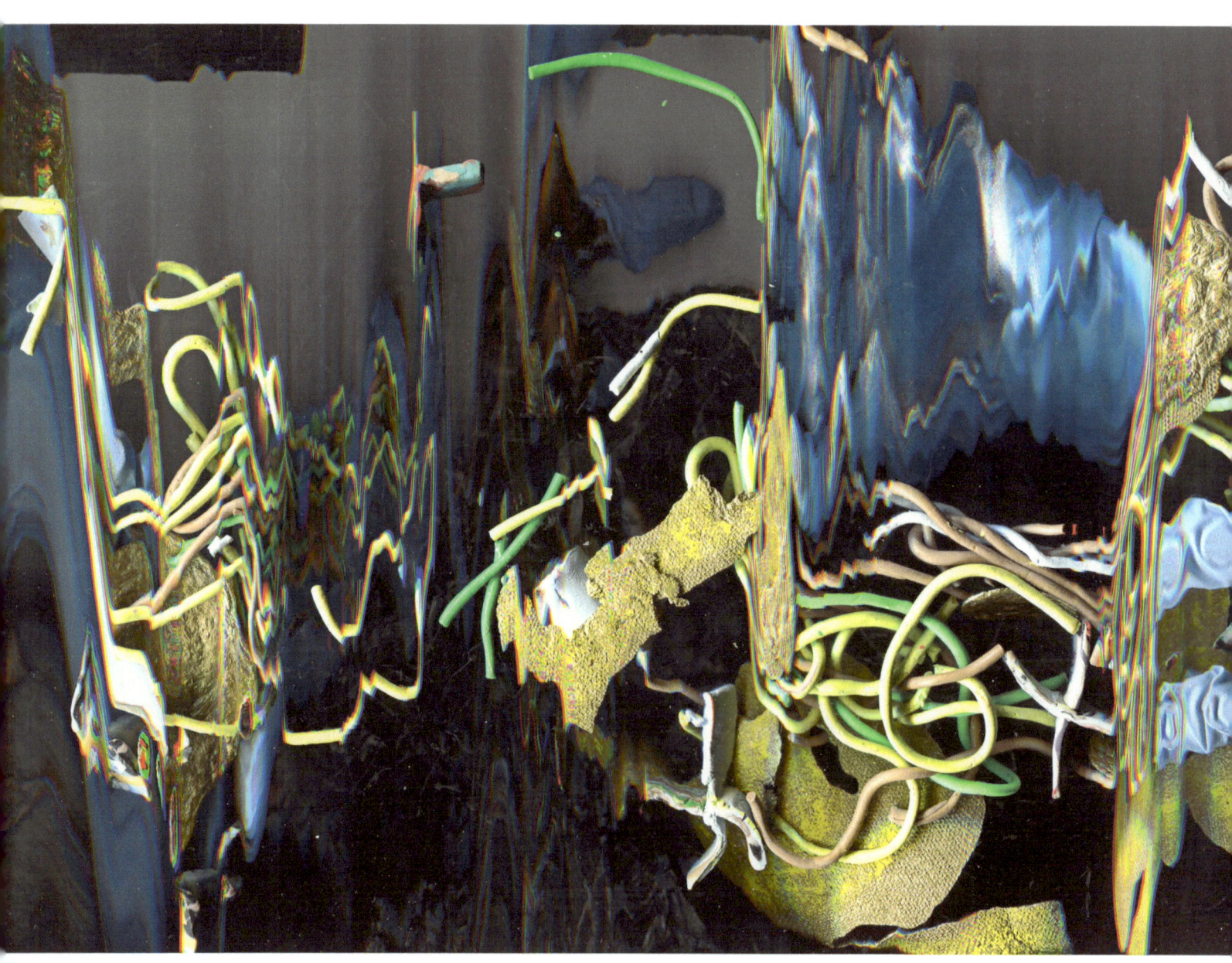

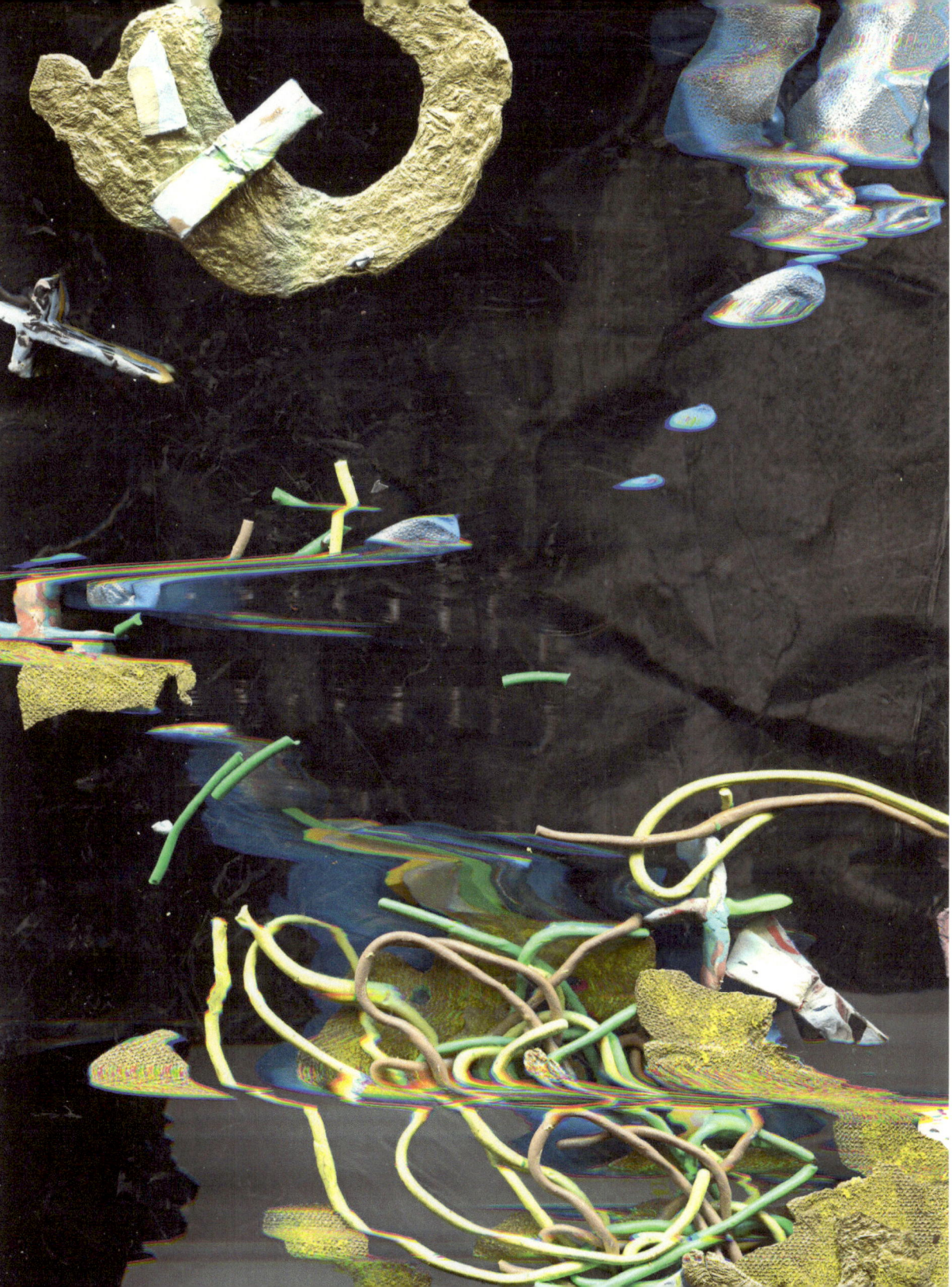

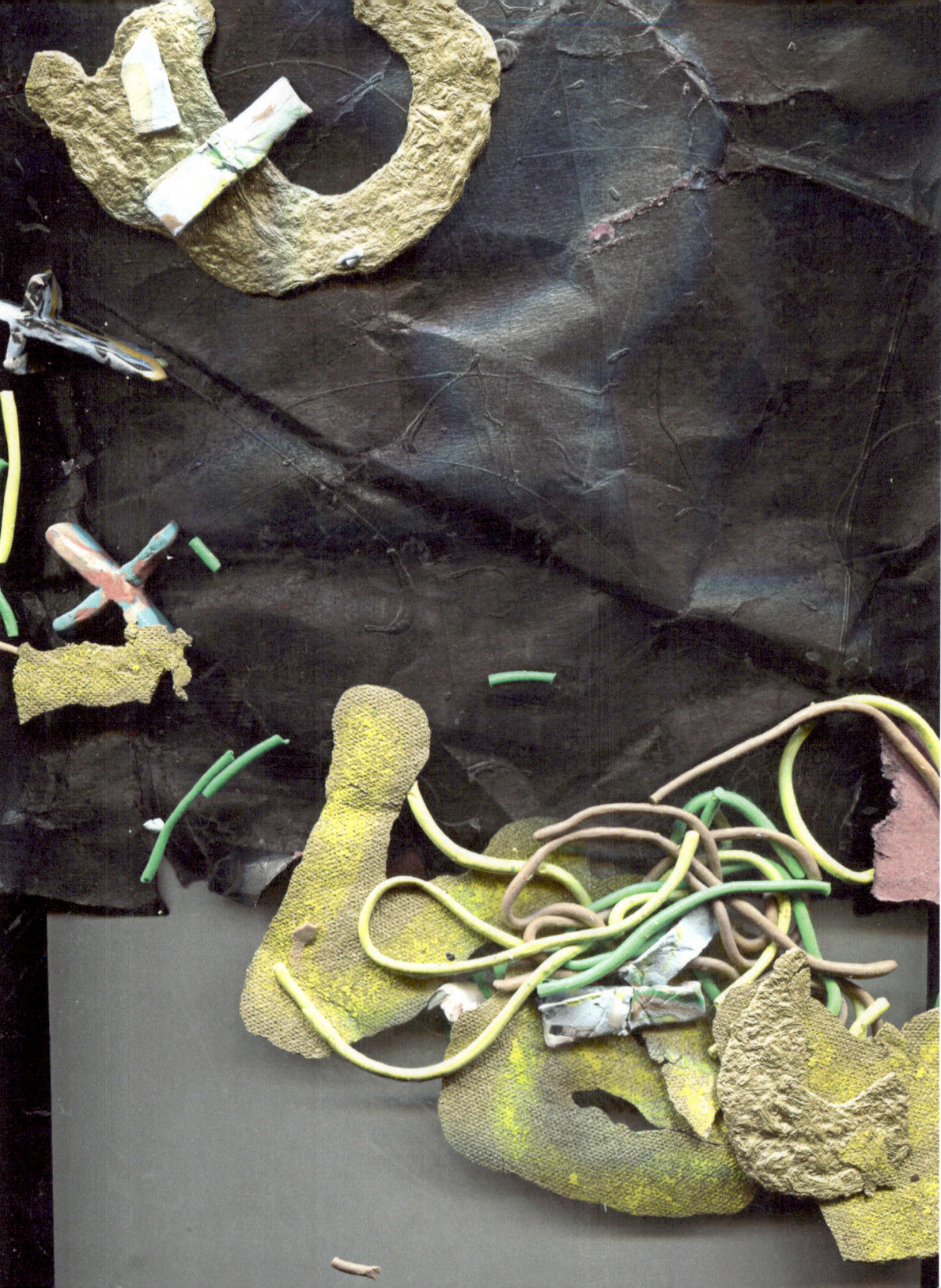

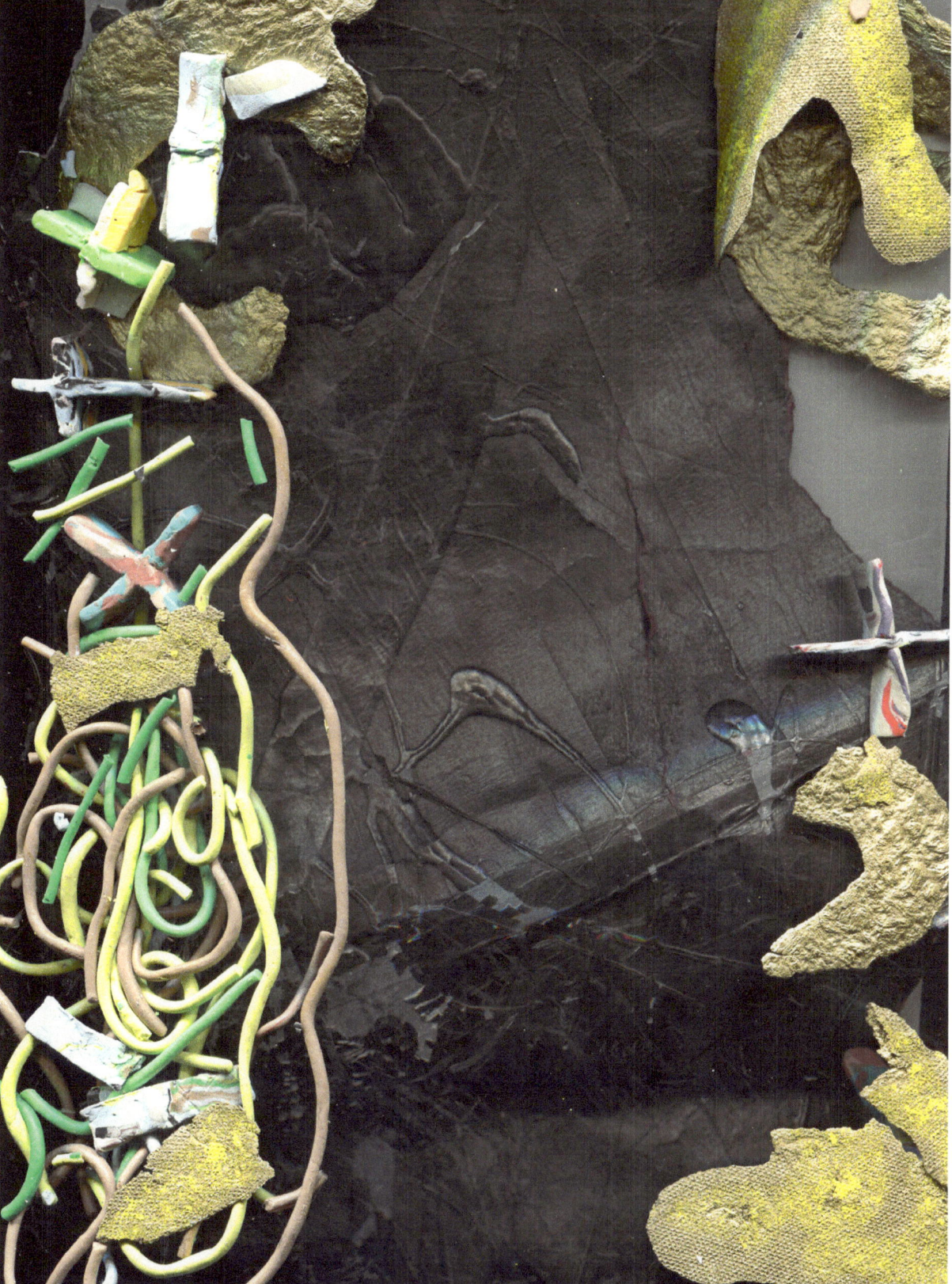

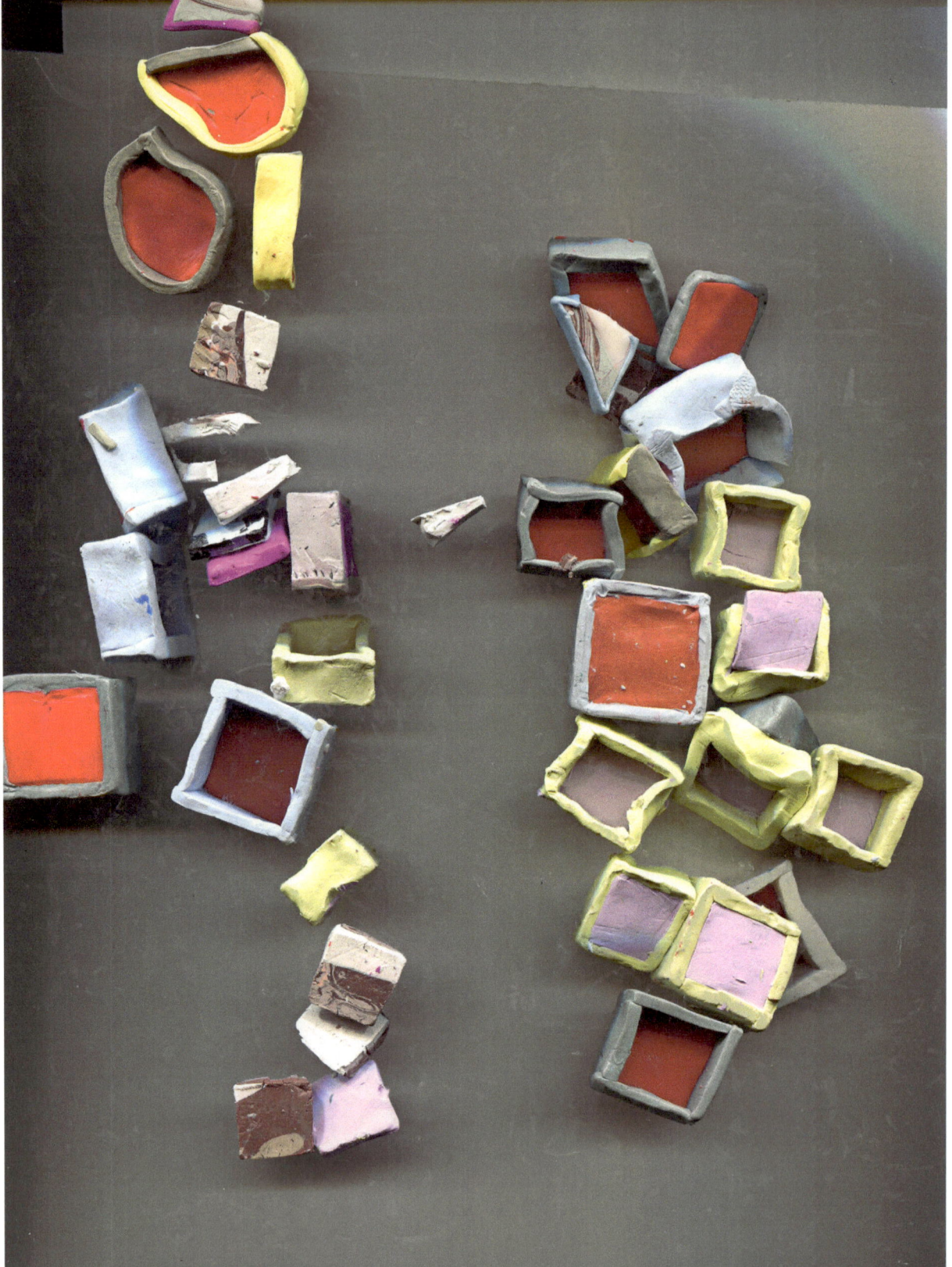

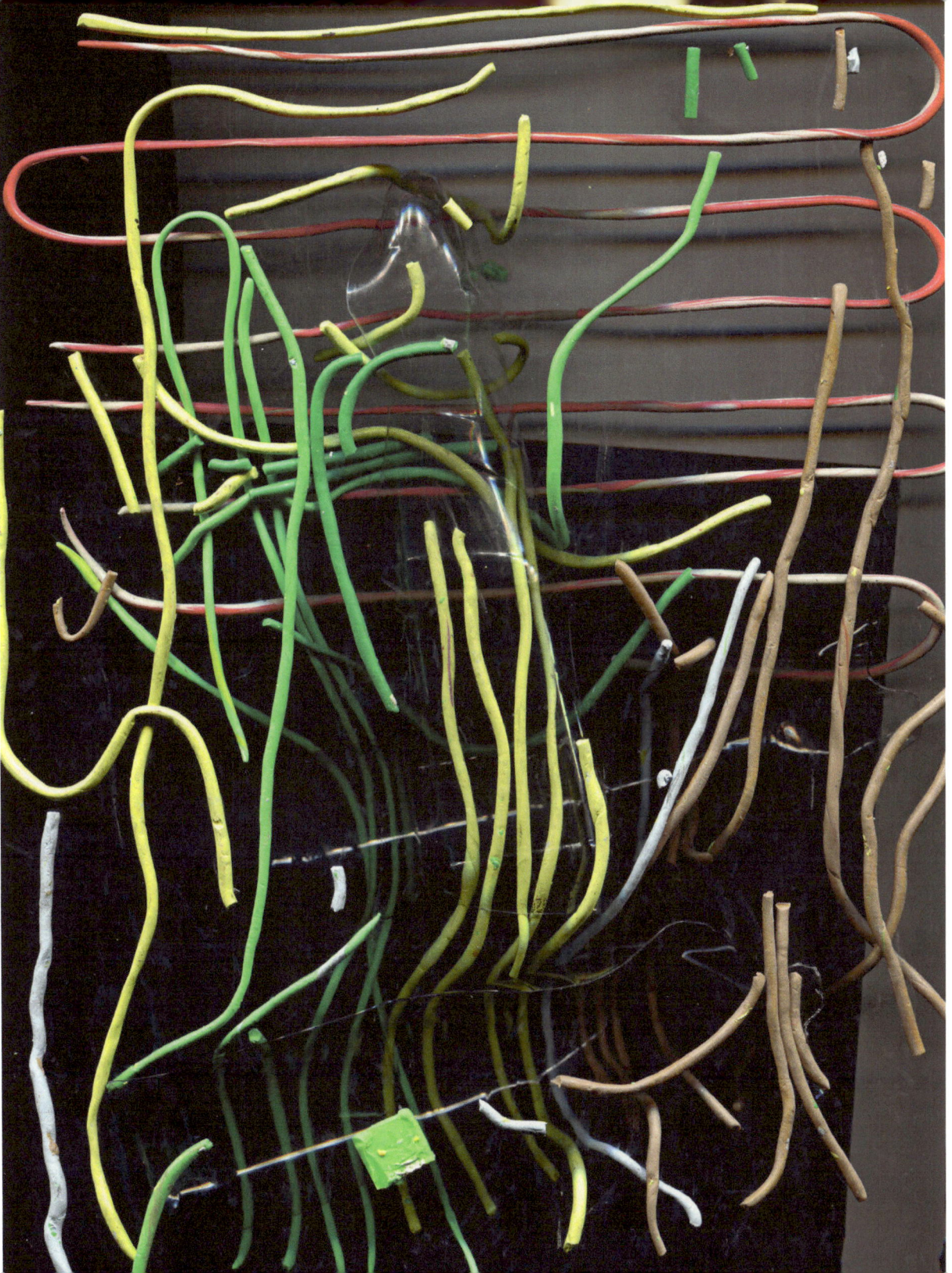

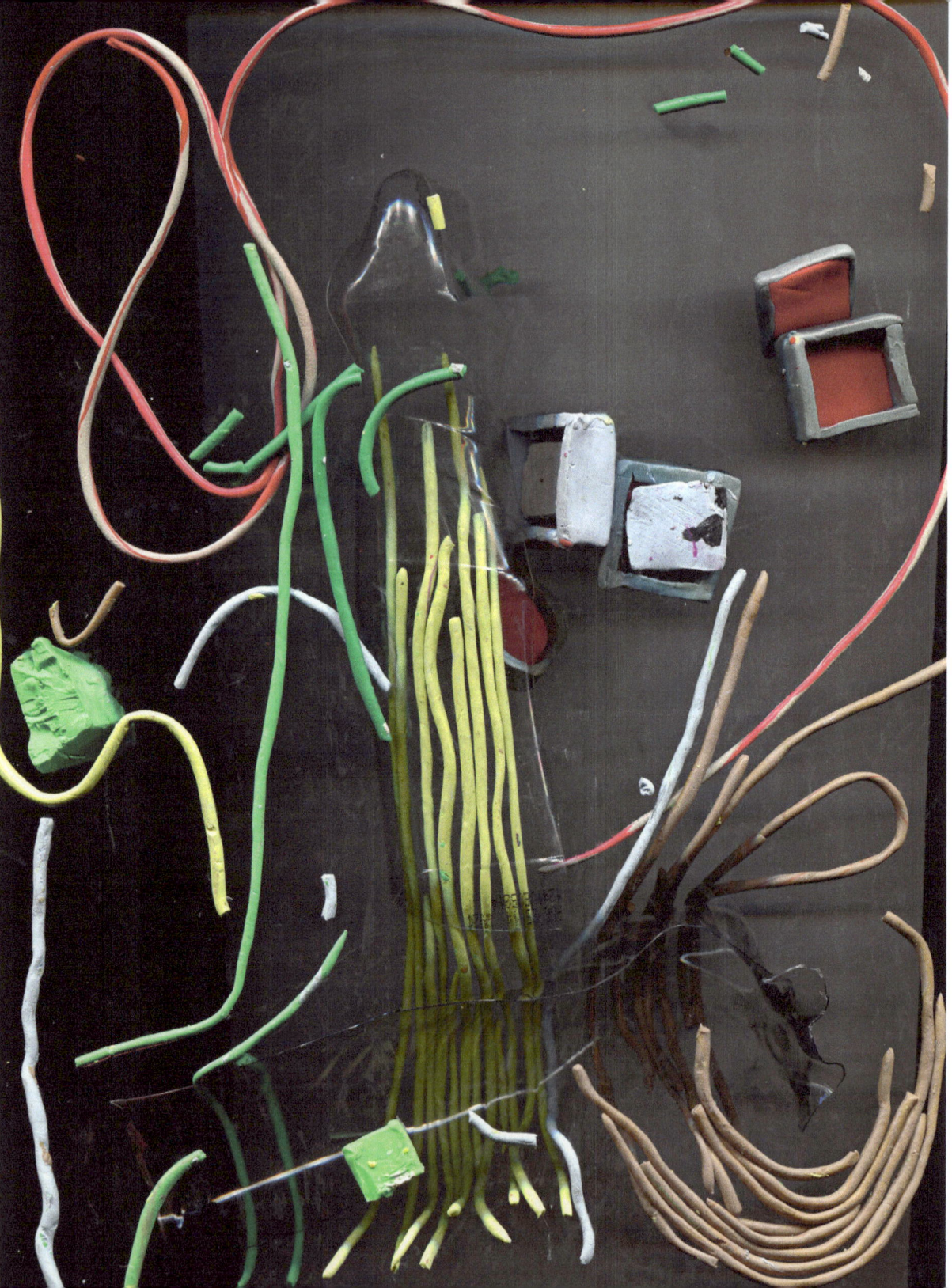

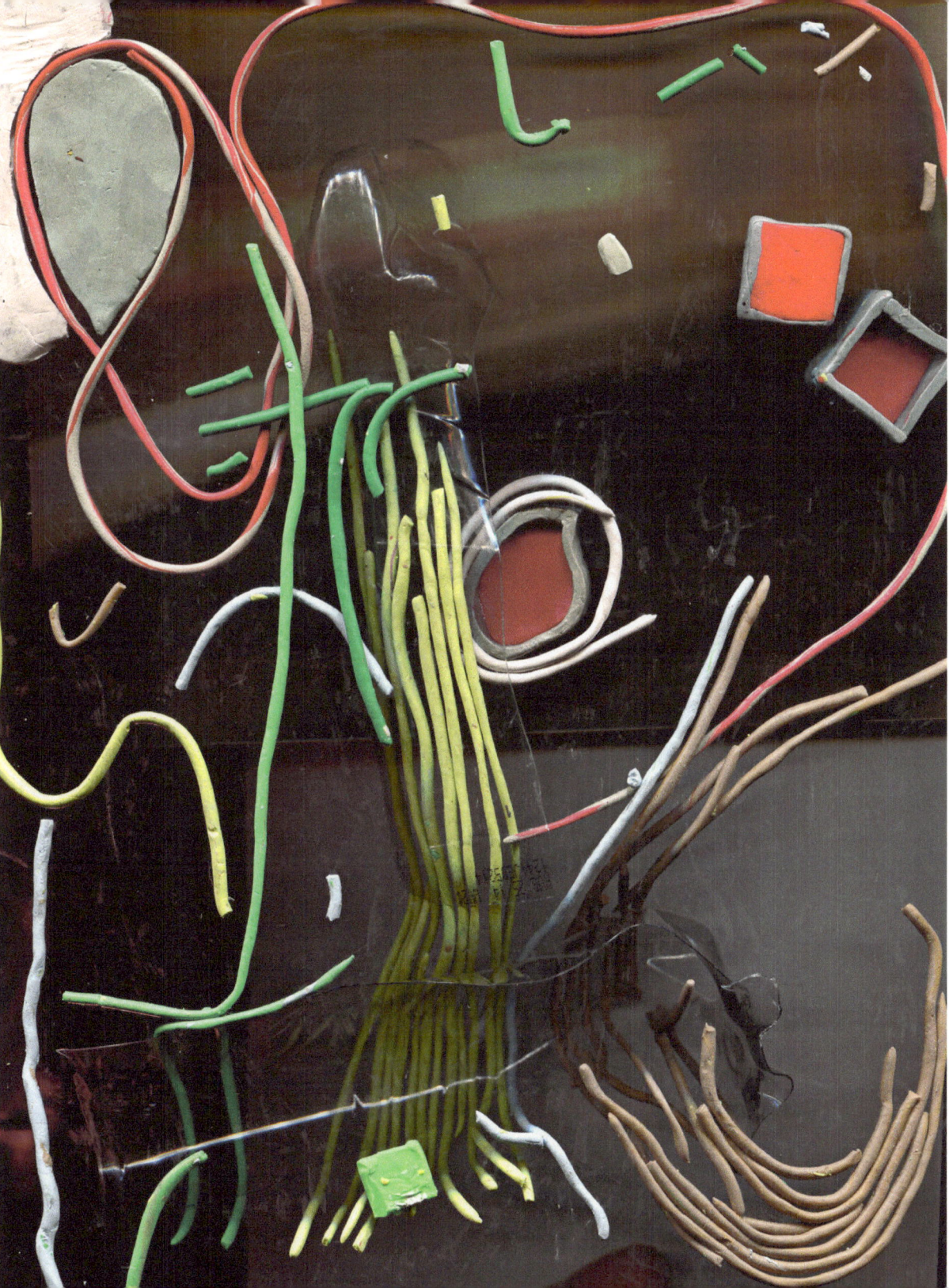

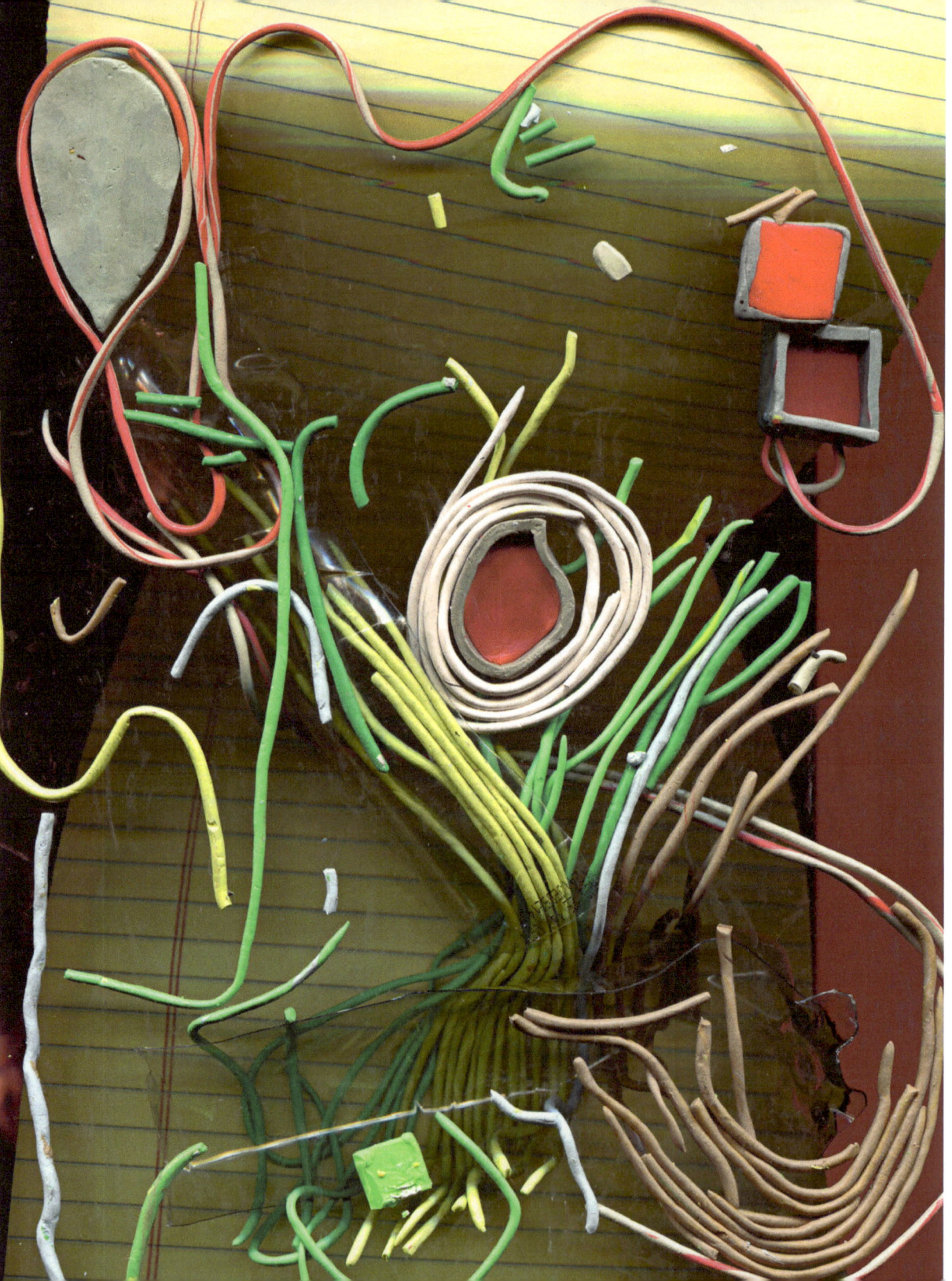

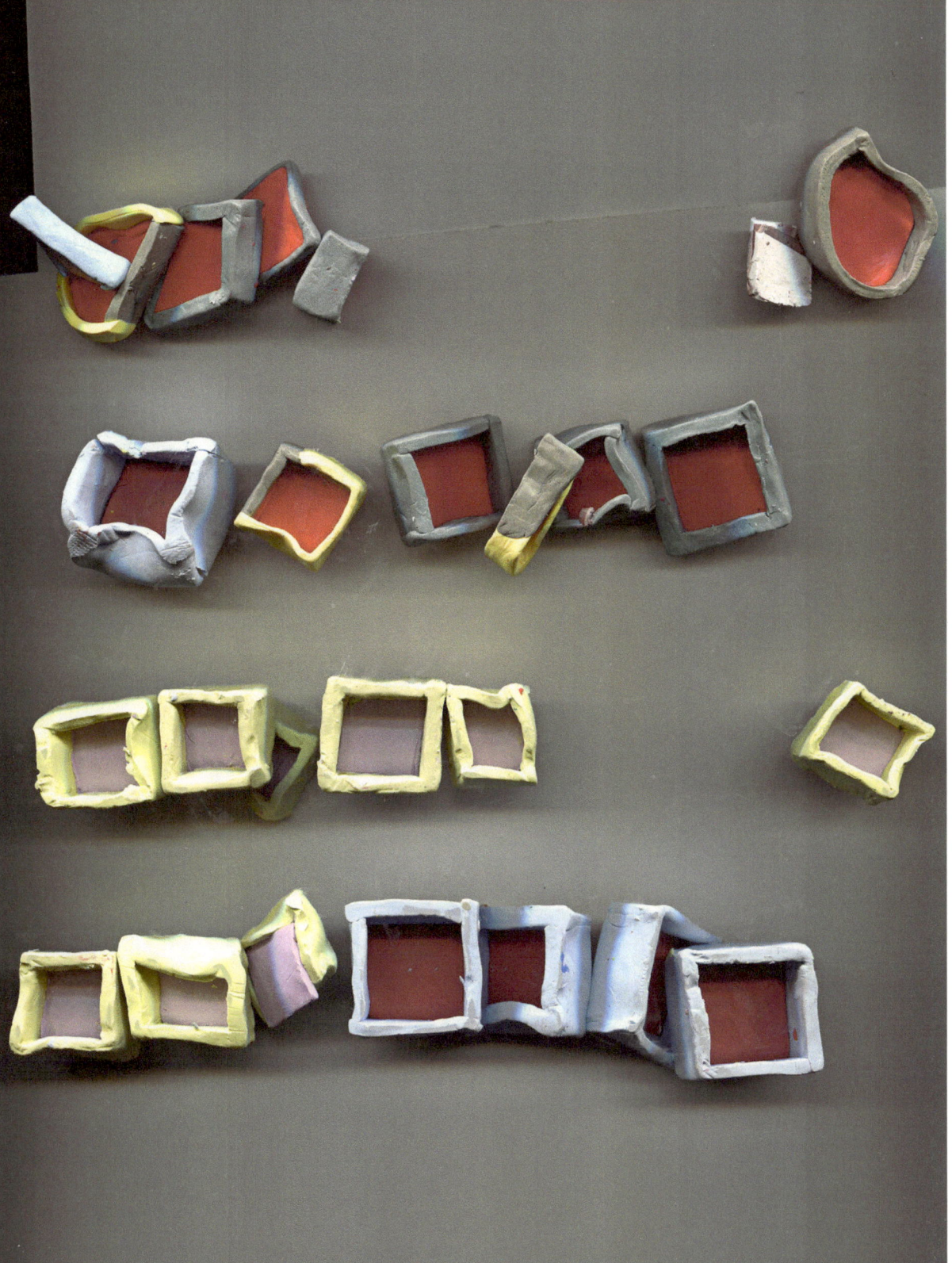

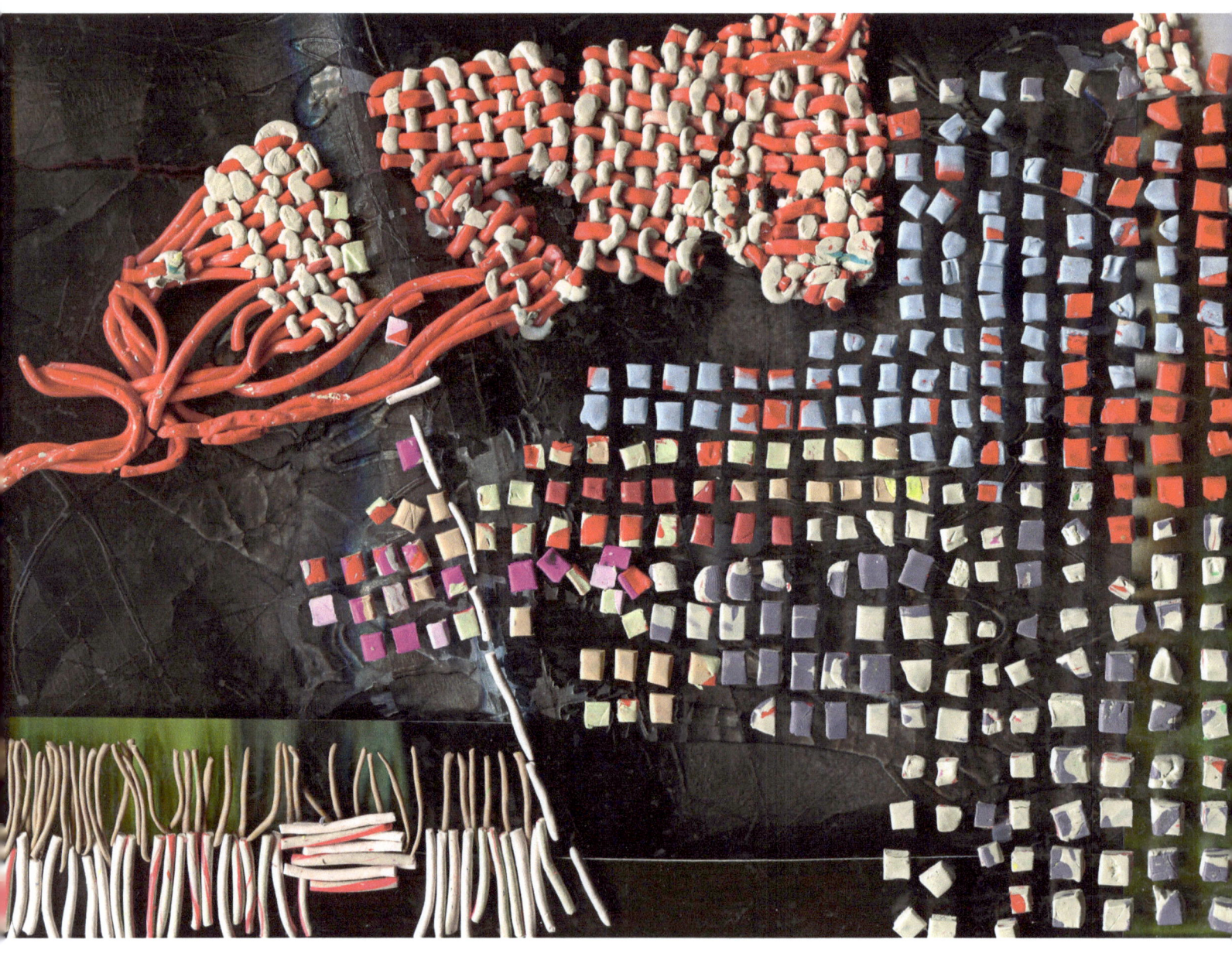

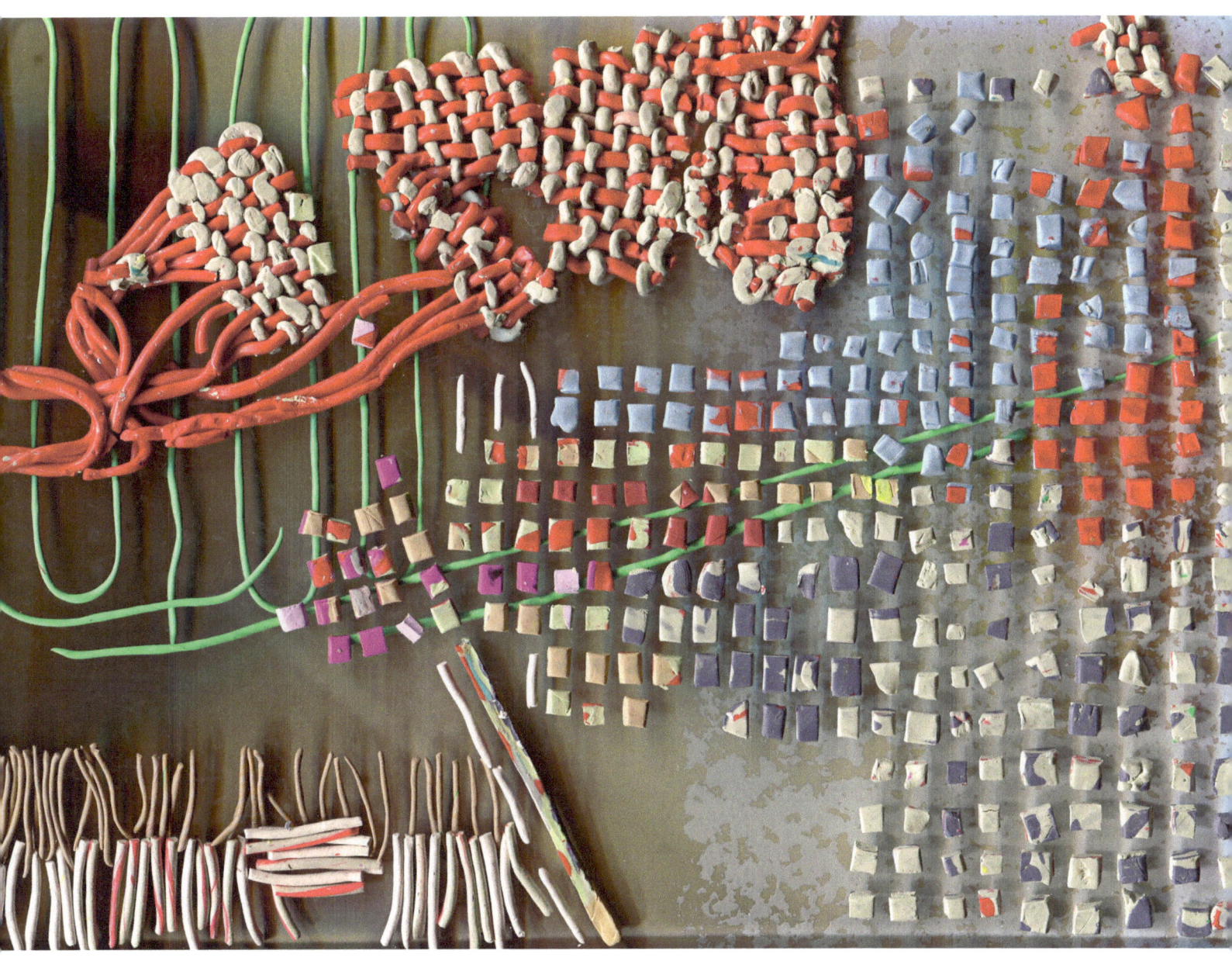

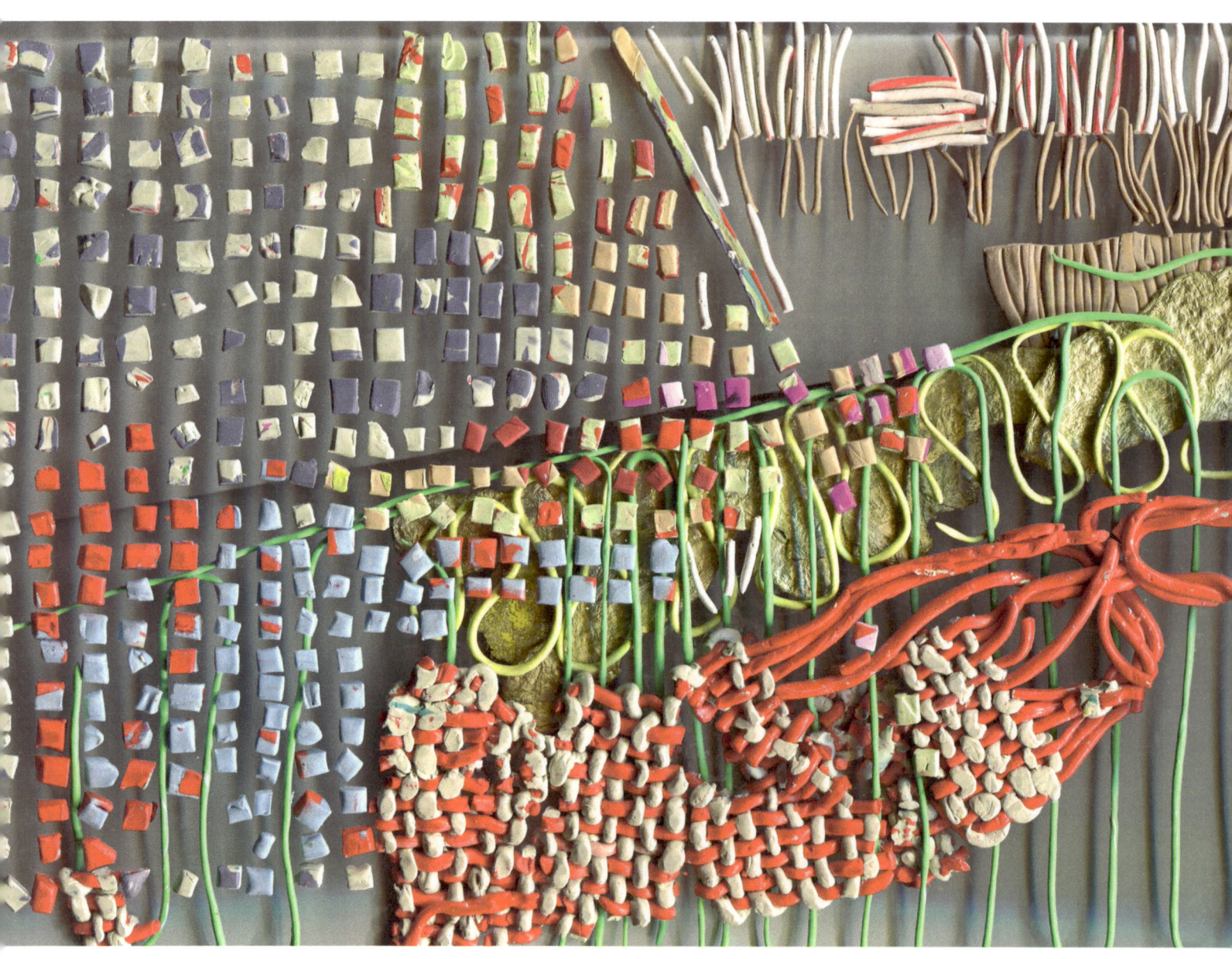

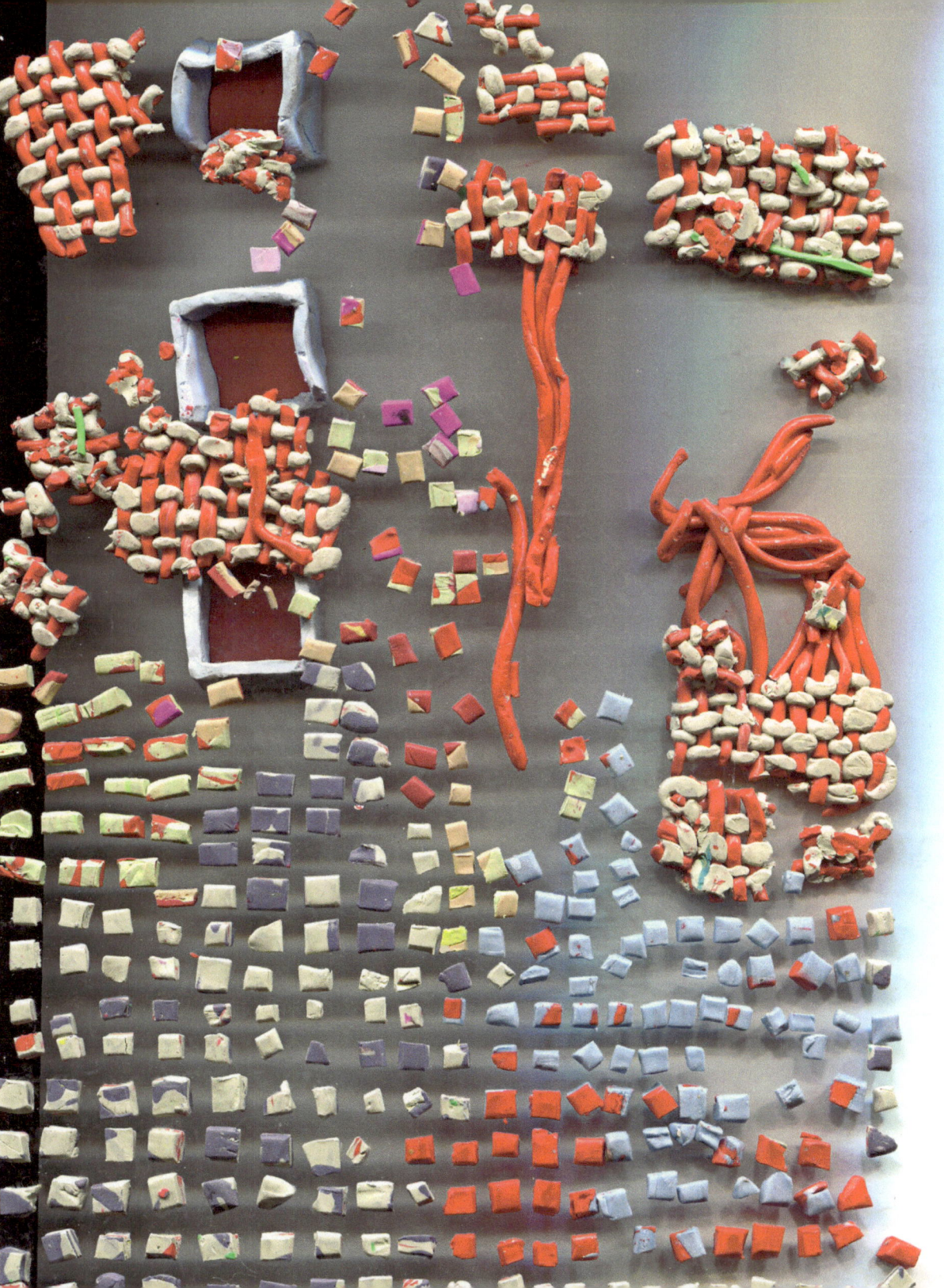

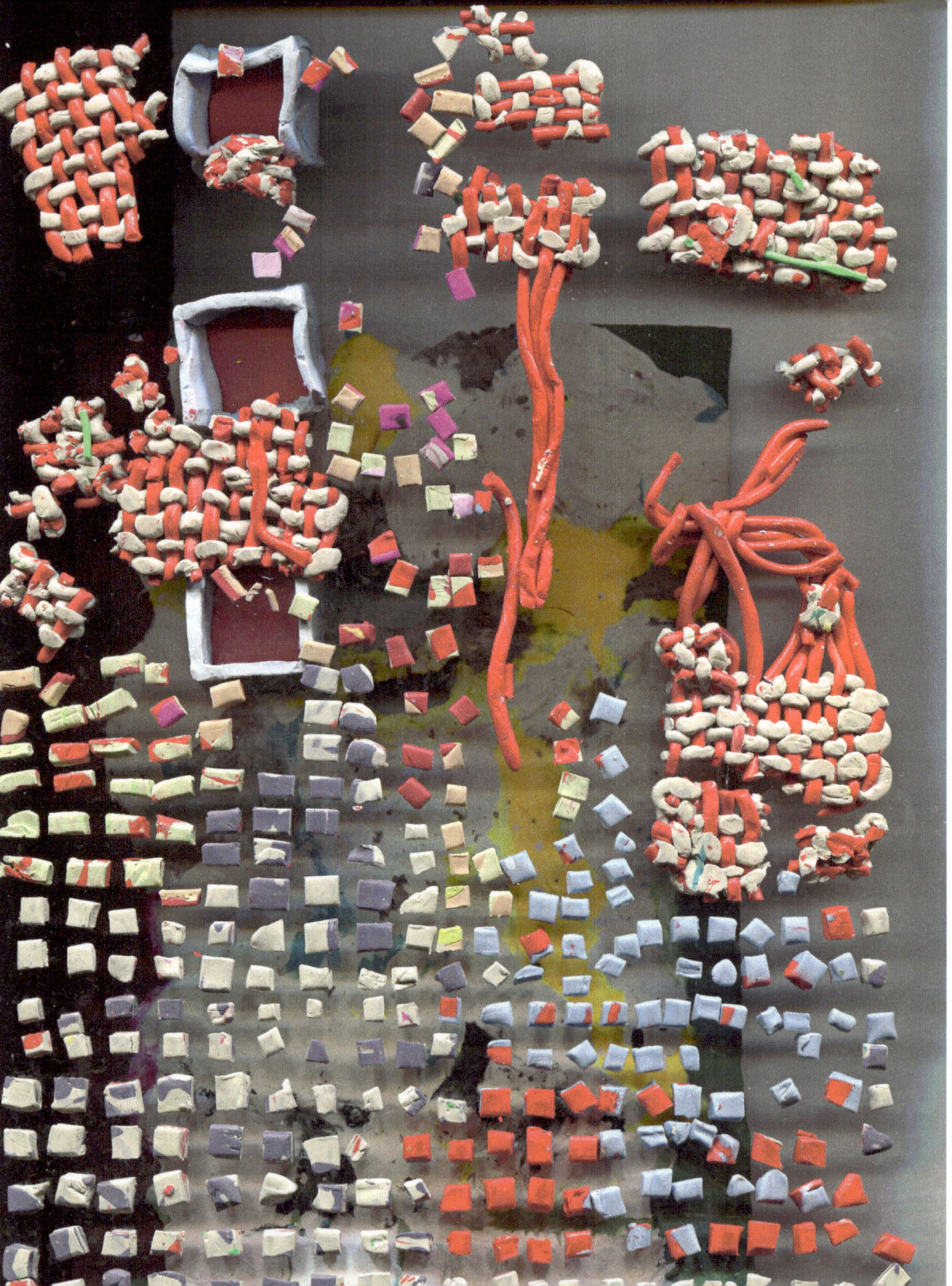

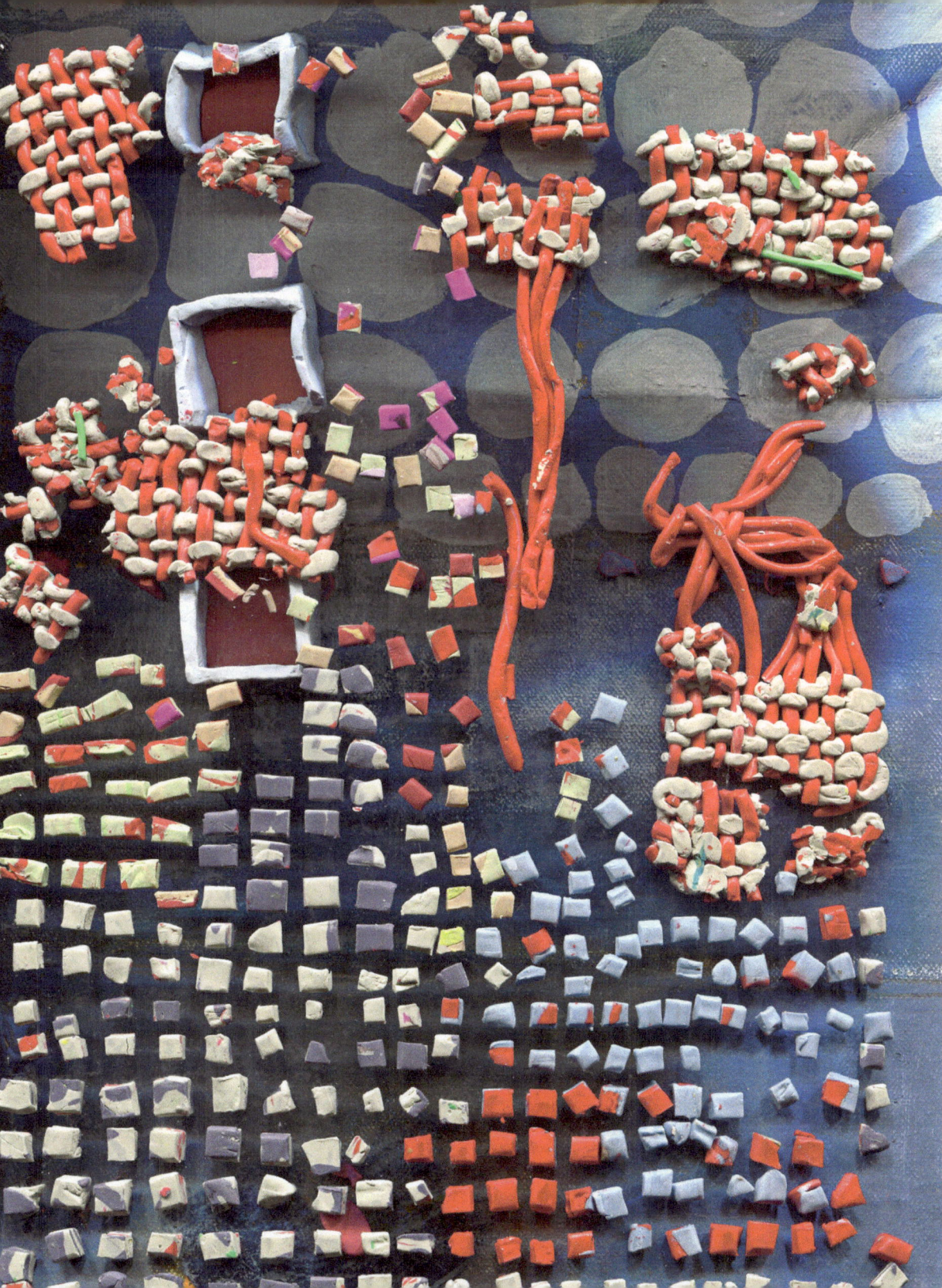

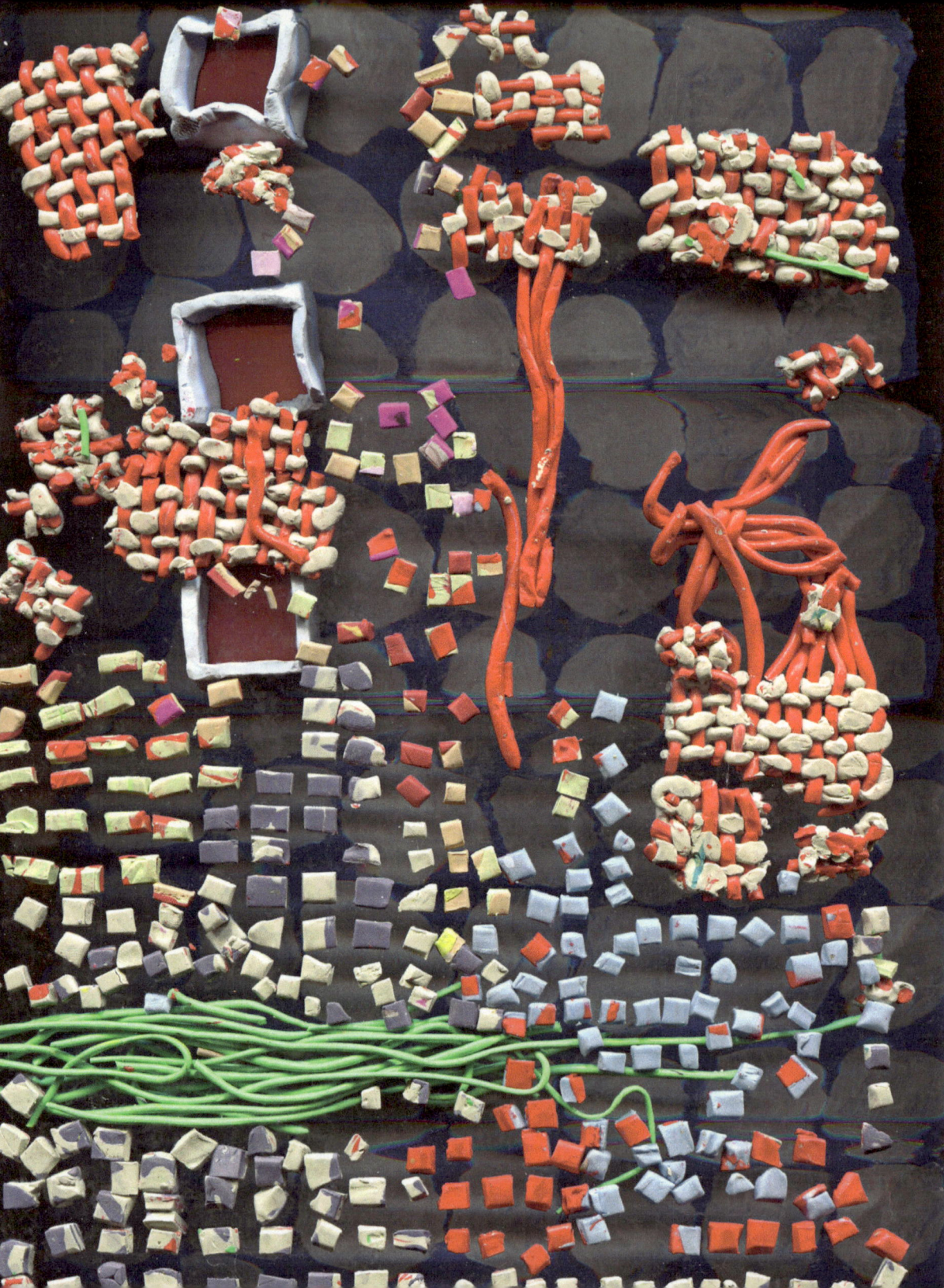

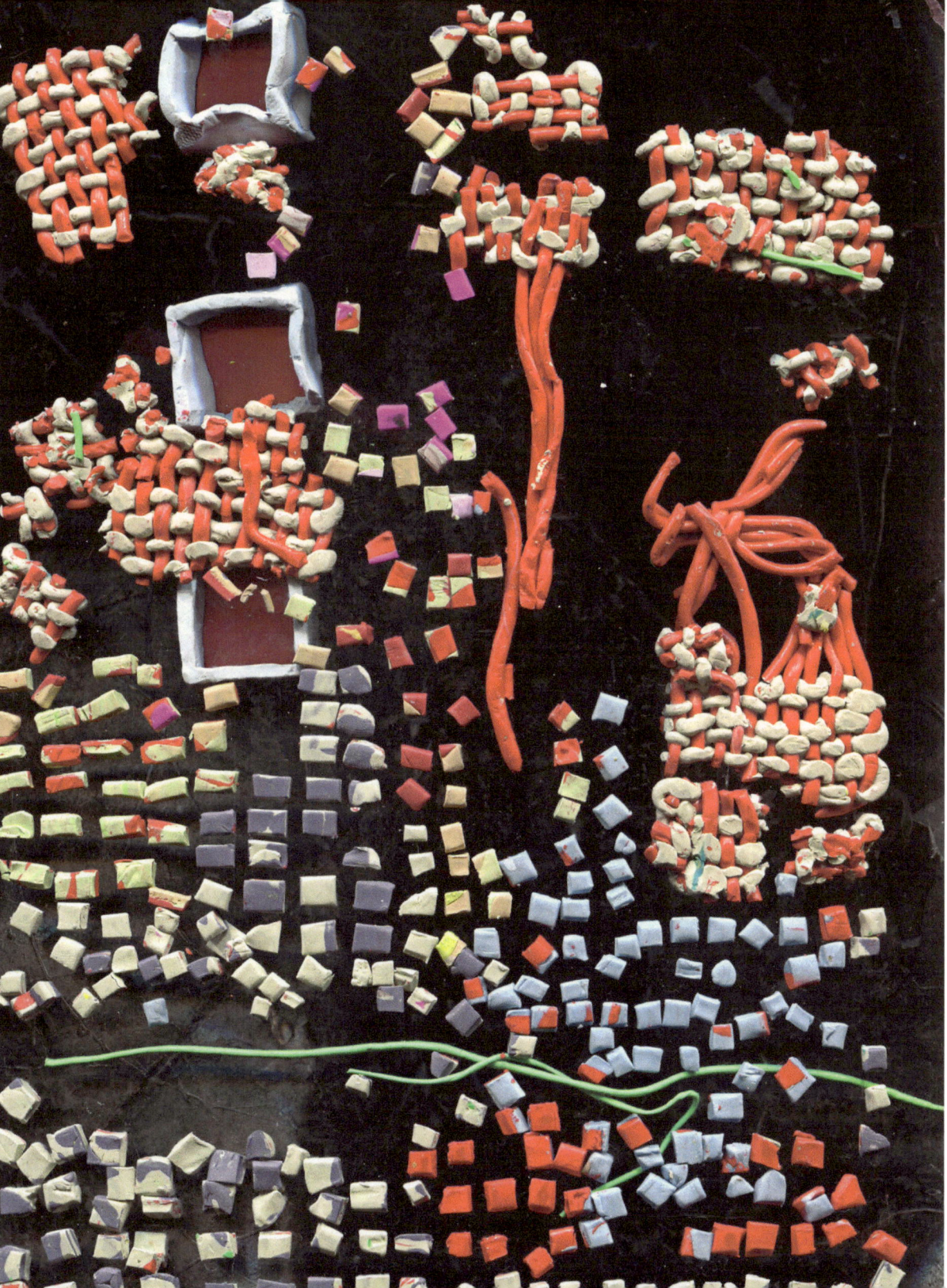

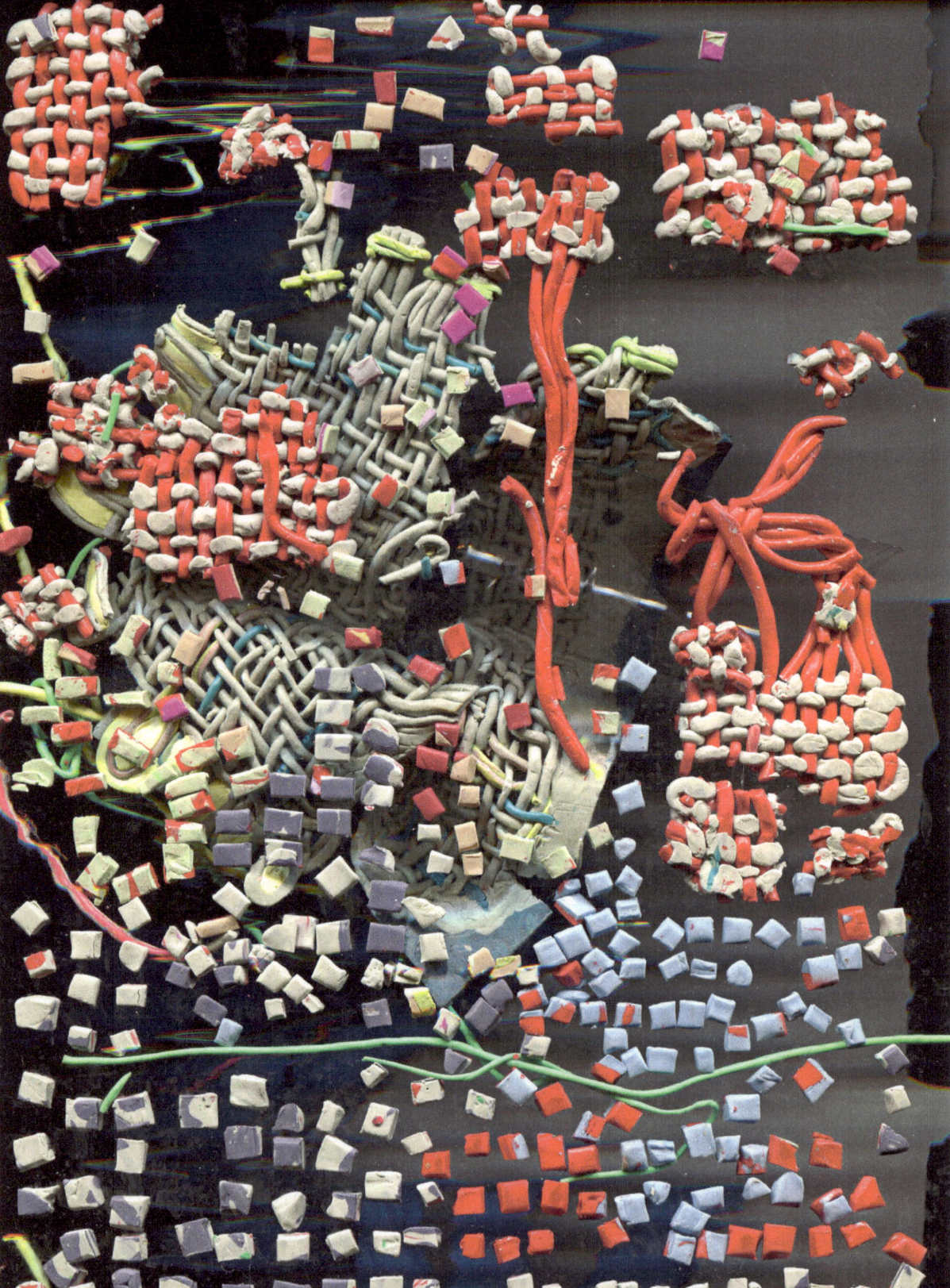

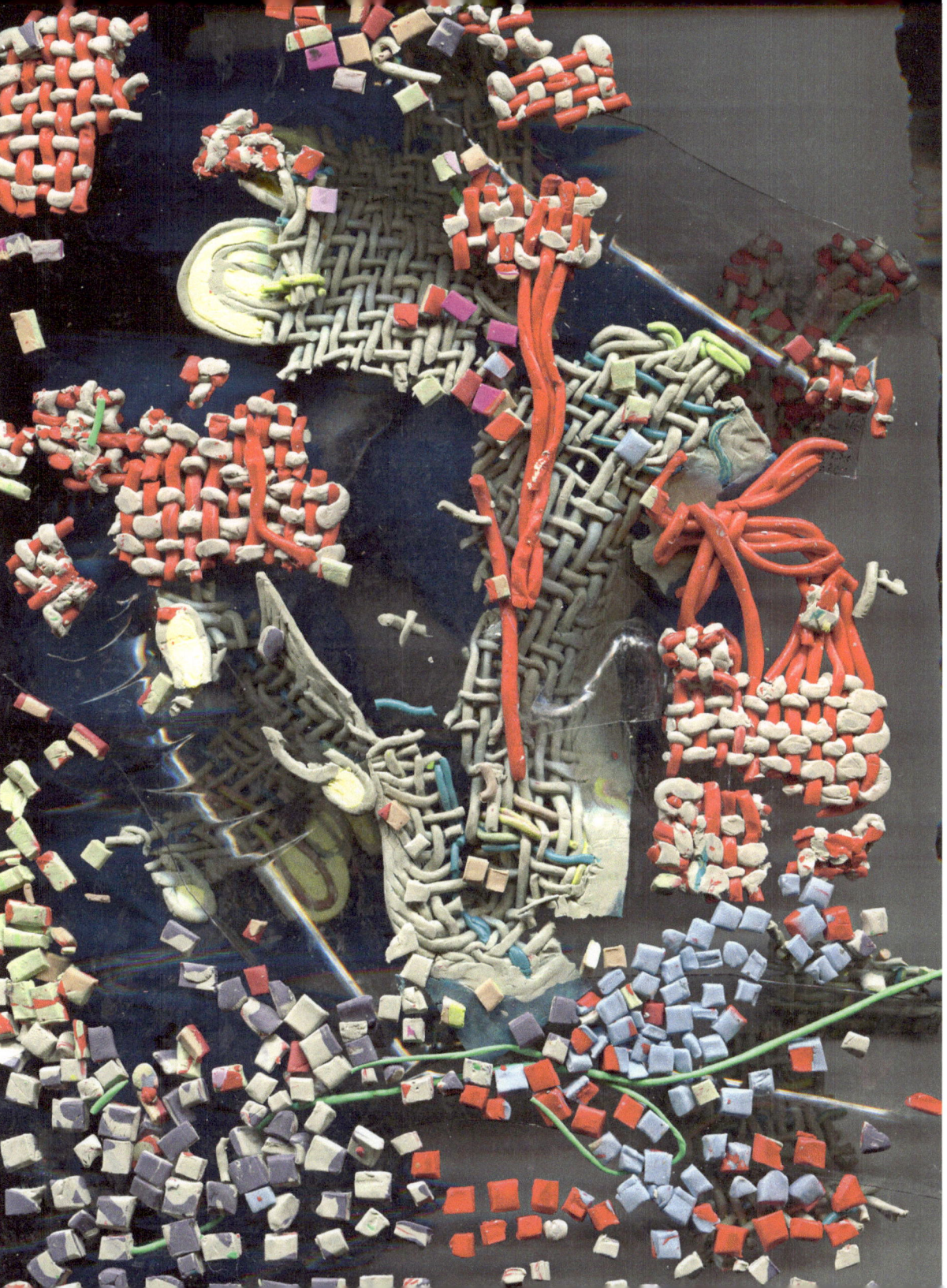

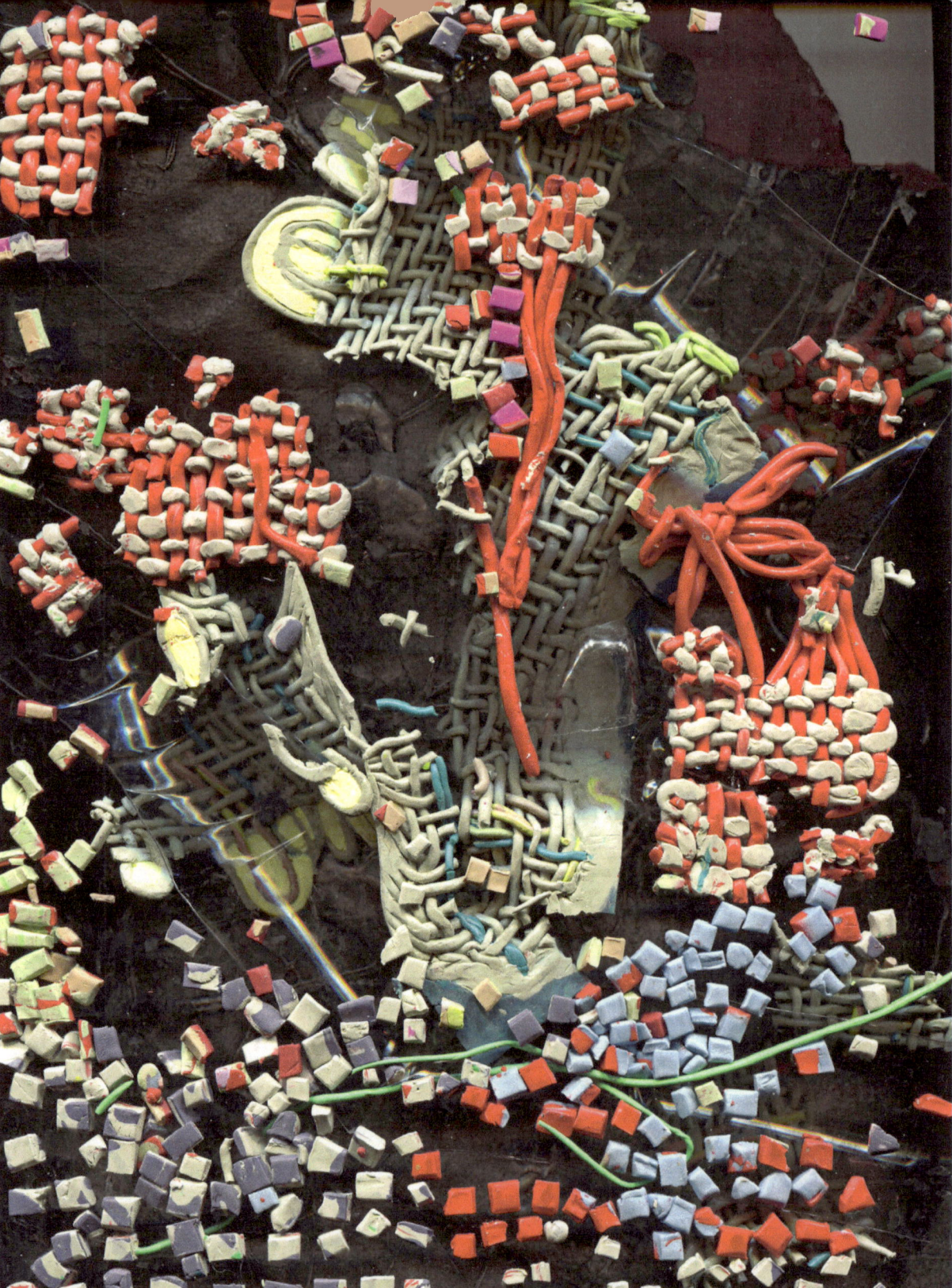

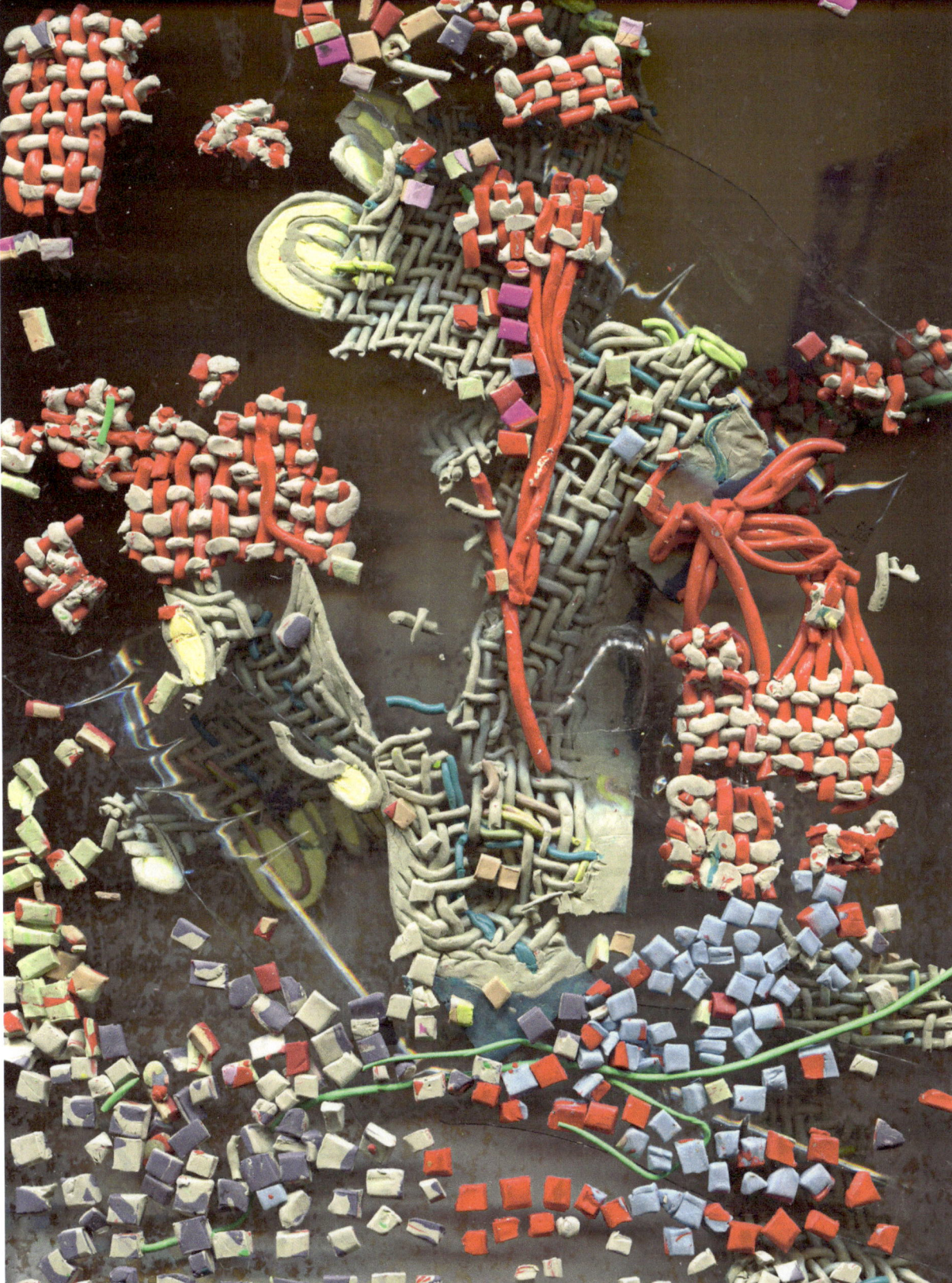

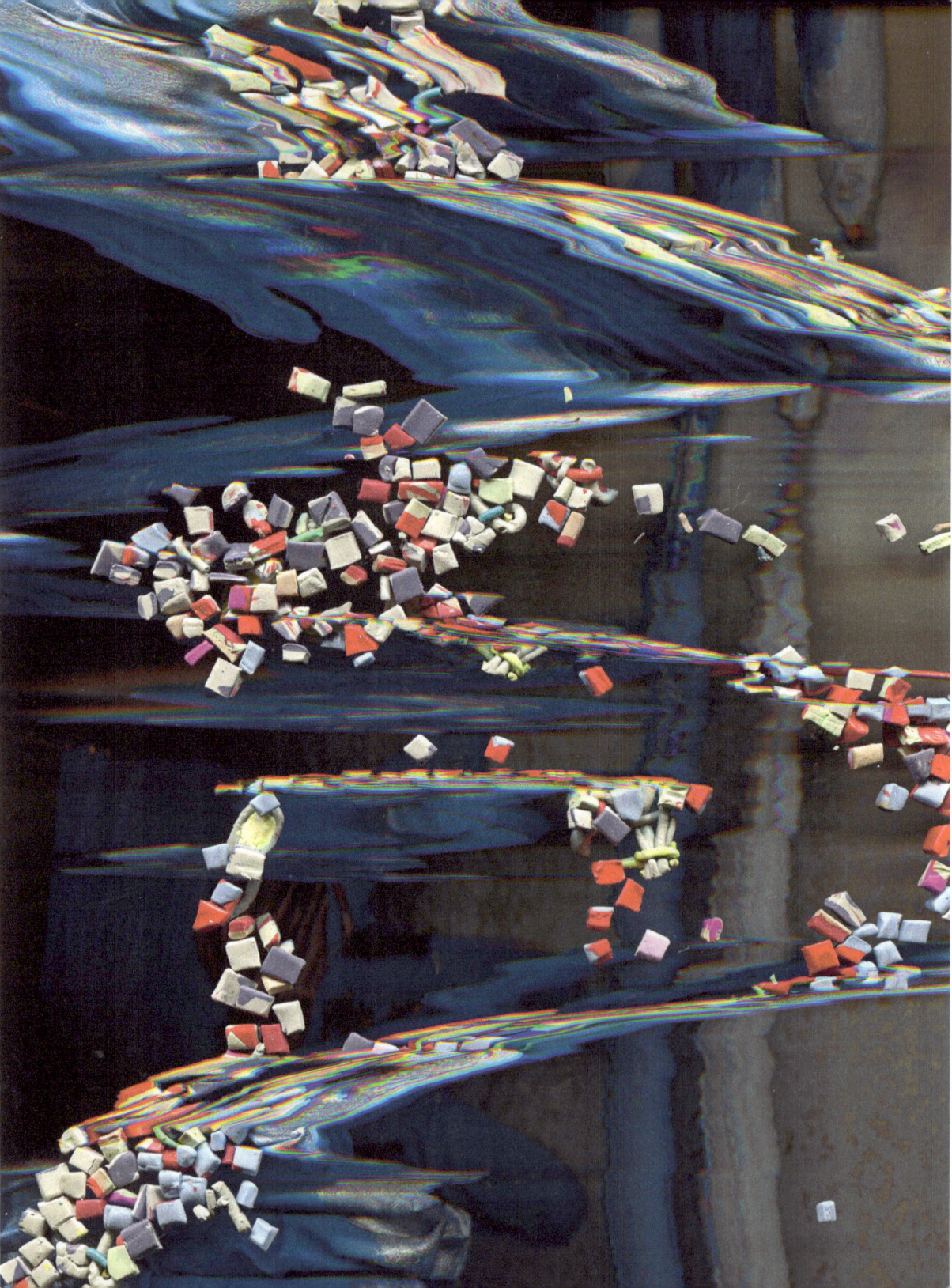

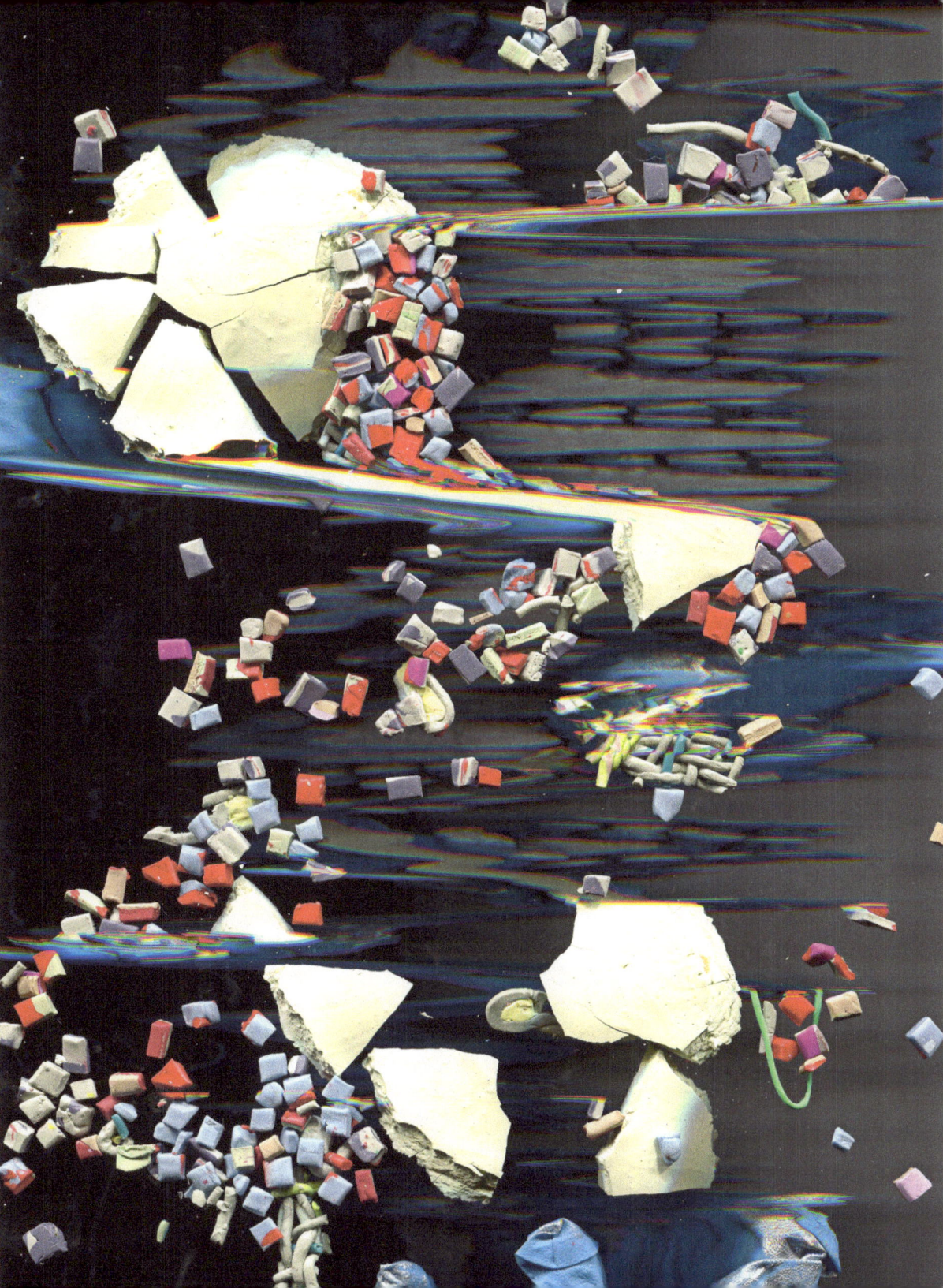

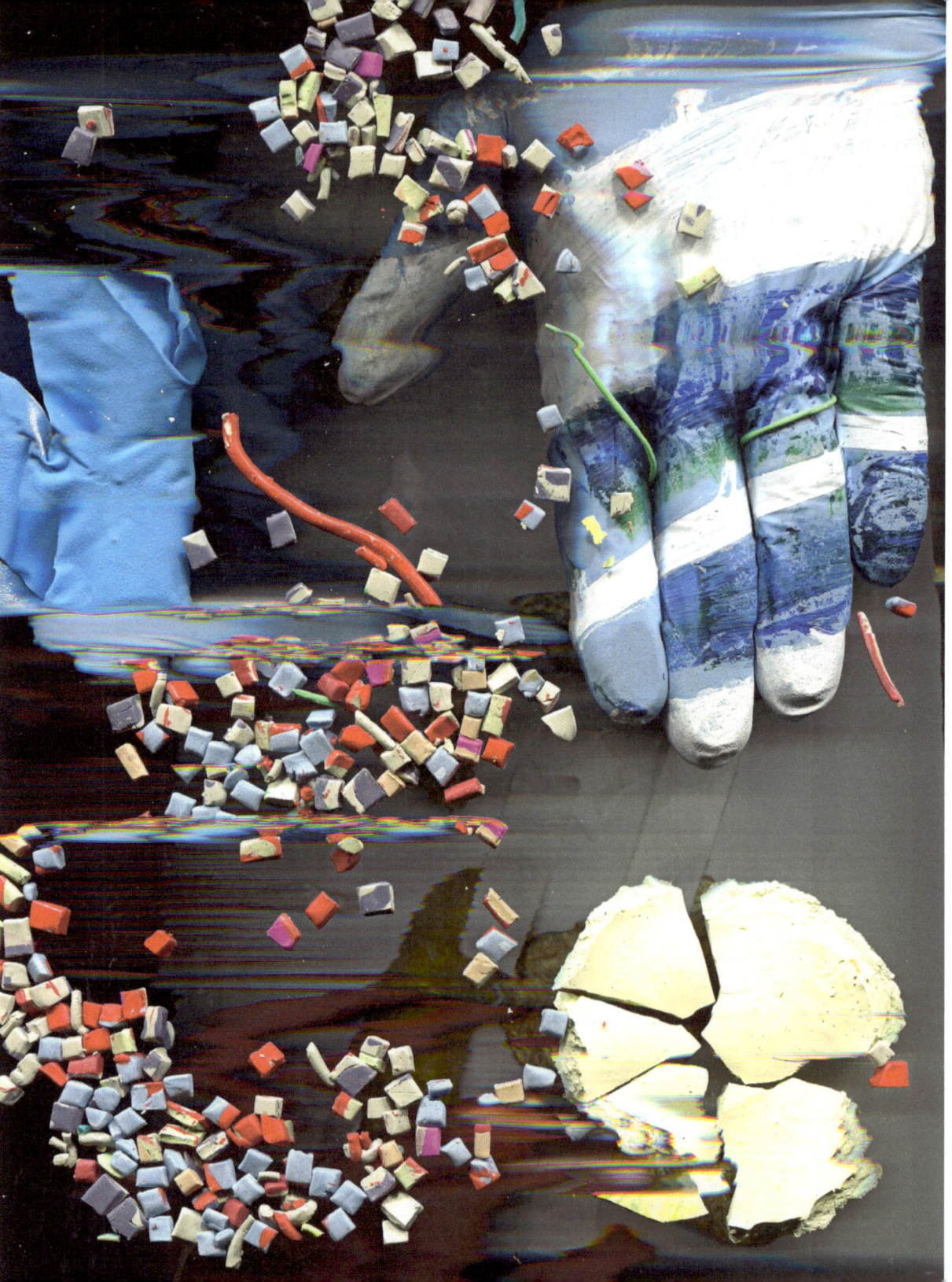

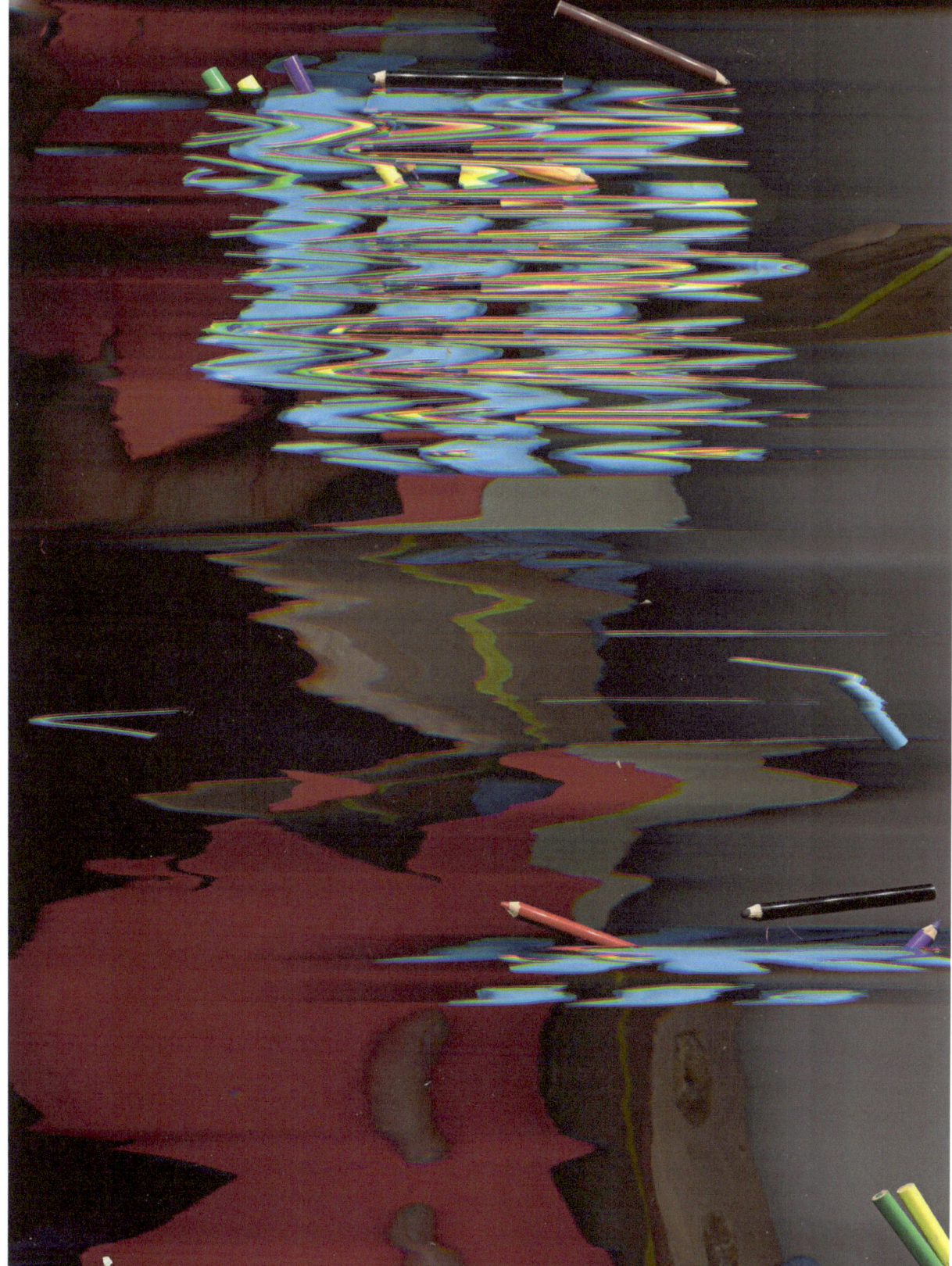

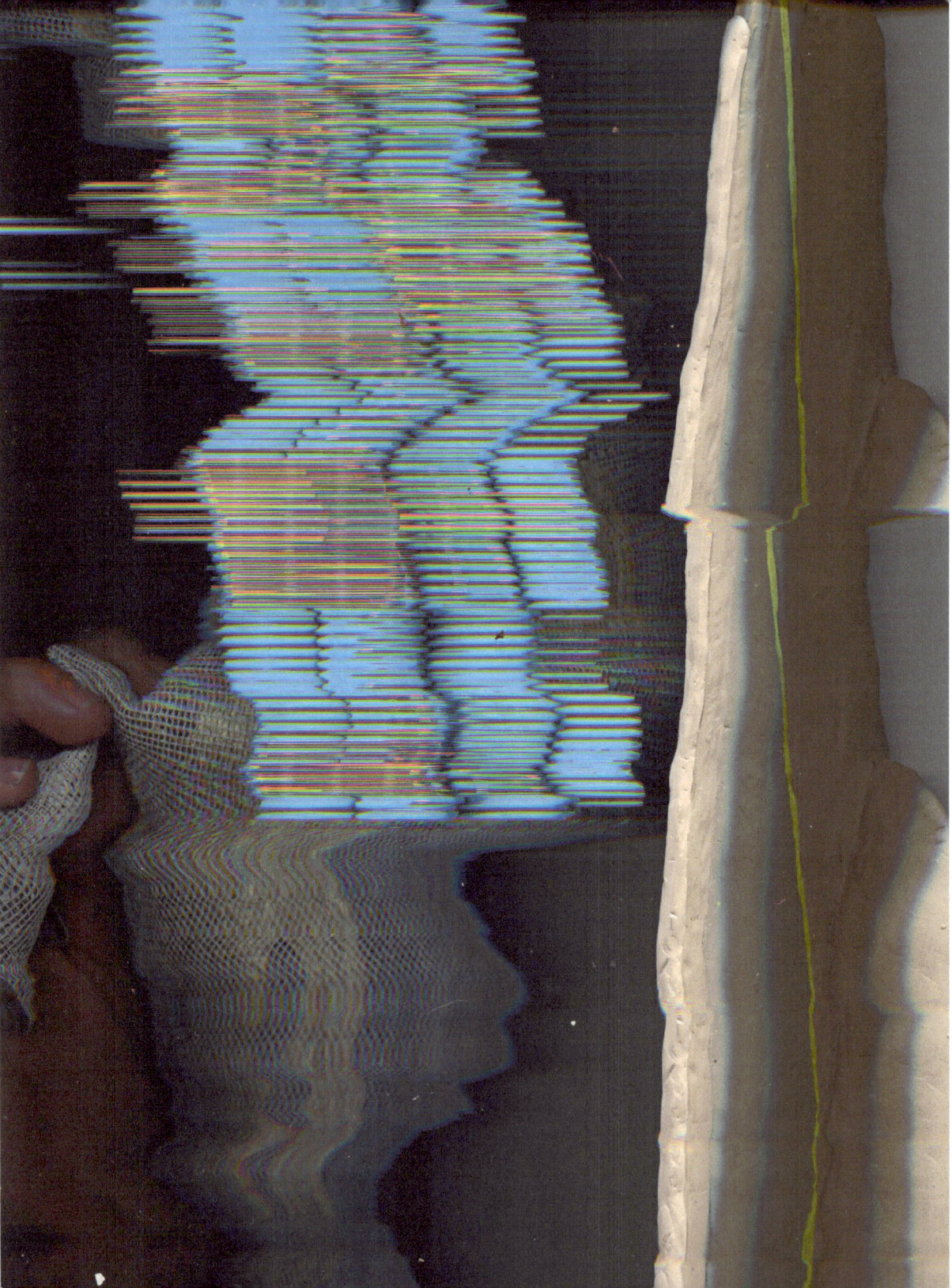

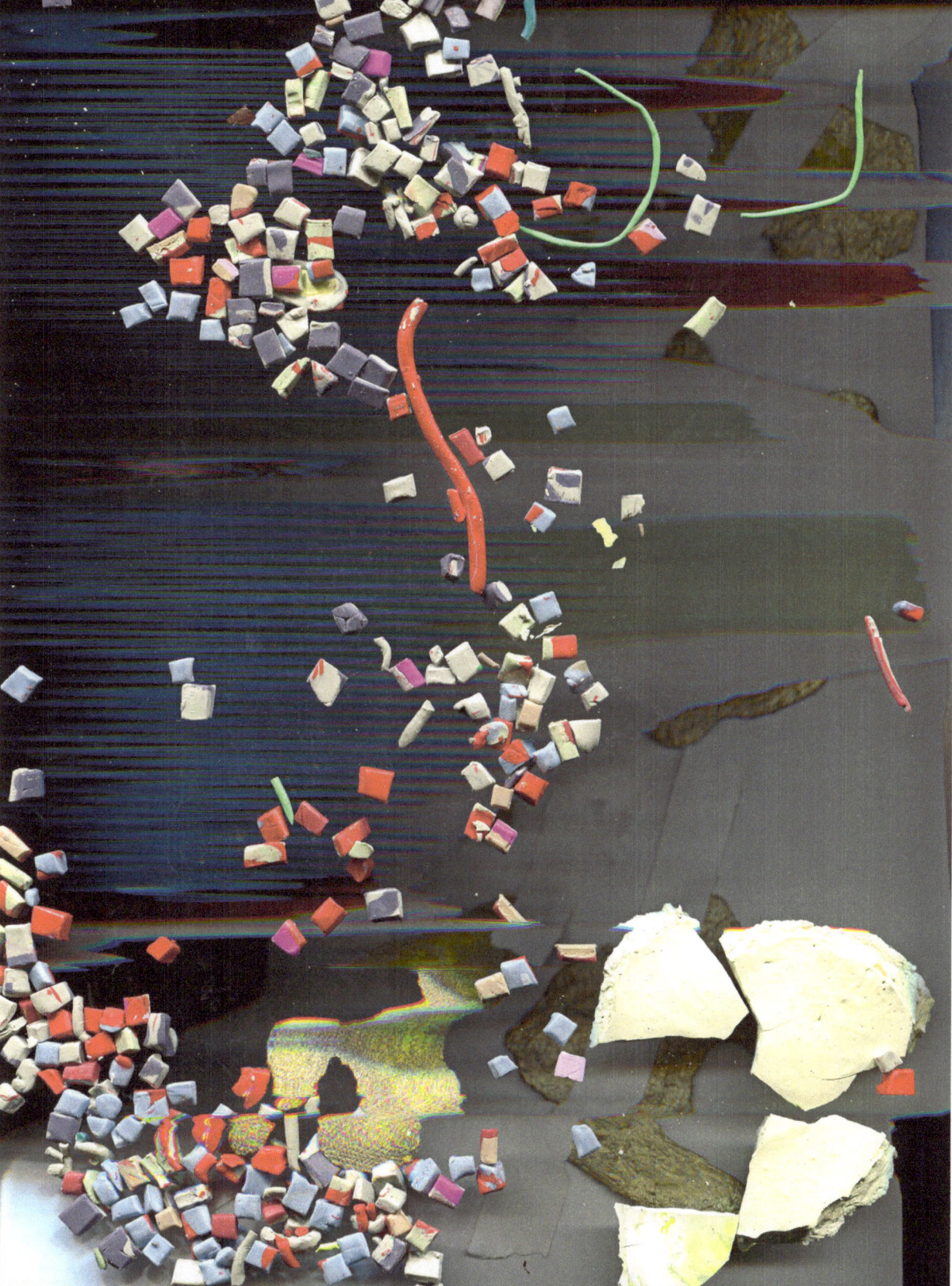

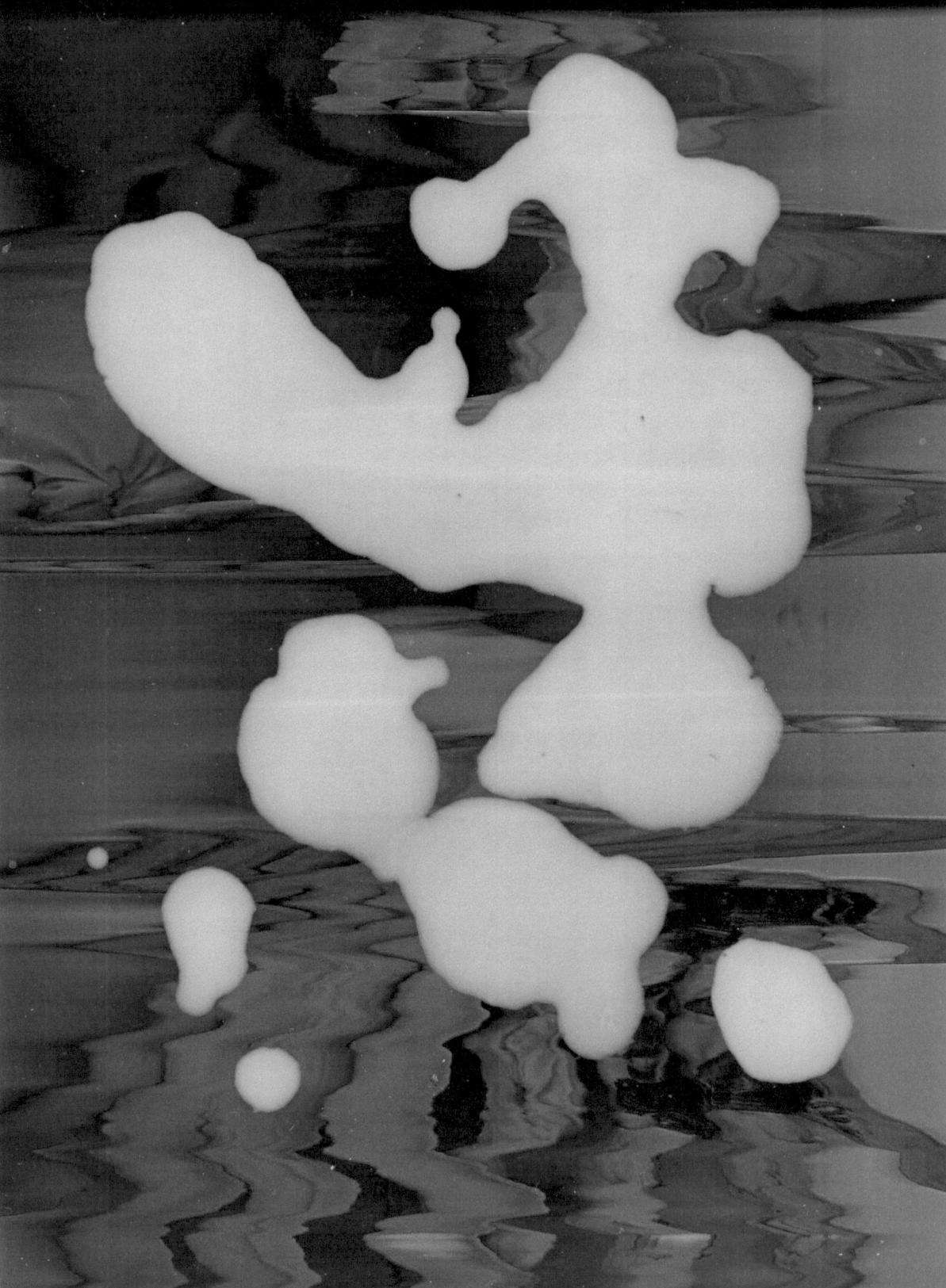